MOVING
MOUNTAINS

Moving Mountains

Stories of faith from the Bible

by

Noelene Martin

Cover design: Mike Ayers
Illustrations: Wendy Carolan

Published by:
National Christian Education Council
Robert Denholm House
Nutfield
Redhill RH1 4HW

British Library Cataloguing-in-Publication Data:
Martin, Noelene
  Moving Mountains.
  1. Bible. Characters
  I. Title
  220.92

ISBN 0-7197-0694-7

First published 1991
© Noelene Martin

Typeset by Avonset, Midsomer Norton, Bath
Printed and bound by the Burlington Press

CONTENTS

		Page
A watchful eye	Exodus 2.1-10	7
Winning the battle	Judges 4.4-23	17
A binding love	Ruth	25
God answers prayer	1 Samuel 1.1-28	33
'I haven't any bread!'	1 Kings 17.8-24	41
The woman who had everything	2 Kings 4.8-37	49
Taking a risk	Esther	59
Through a hole in the roof	Mark 2.1-12	83
The healing touch	Mark 5.25-34	93
'I've so much to do!'	Luke 10.38-42	101
By the pool	John 5.1-18	109
Not on the Sabbath	Luke 13.10-17	115
'I've found it!'	Luke 15.8-10	121
The generous gift	Mark 12.41-44	129
'I can see!'	John 9.1-39	135
'If only you'd been here . . .'	John 11.1-44	145
An expensive waste	John 12.1-8	153
The Lord is risen!	John 20.1-18	159
Part of a team	Acts 18.1-28	171

A watchful eye

For many years, the Egyptians and the people of Israel had lived together in Egypt. But when a new king – or 'Pharaoh' – became ruler, he wasn't happy with the situation. He found that the Israelites were having more children than the Egyptians!

'If this continues', he thought, 'there will be so many Israelites in this country that they will take over the land.'

The Pharaoh didn't want this to happen so he ordered that all the Israelites were to become slaves. They had to work for long hours every day for their Egyptian masters, making buildings and working in the fields and houses of the Egyptians. They were whipped and treated cruelly, and their lives were very unhappy. But, in spite of this, the Israelite families still continued to grow.

The Pharaoh became more and more worried – and then very angry. What could he do now? How could he get rid of all these Israelites? He thought hard and then smiled as an evil plan entered his head.

'Whenever a baby boy is born to an Israelite woman,' he told his people, 'take him and throw him into the river!'

The Israelites were horrified when they heard what the Pharaoh had commanded. Now, instead of happiness when a baby boy was born, there was fear, sadness and crying. Some mothers tried to hide their babies from the Egyptians but it was very difficult. The soldiers would search their homes and find the hidden baby, taking no notice of the tears and entreaties of the baby's family.

However, one mother was determined to save her baby son. Every time Egyptian soldiers came near, she hid him, hoping desperately that he wouldn't cry. For three months she kept him secret, always watchful and fearful that he would be found. But she realised she couldn't hide him forever – he was growing older and stayed awake longer during the day. Whatever could she do?

One morning Miriam, the woman's daughter, came into the kitchen and found her mother kneeling on the floor. In front of her was a large woven basket and some black sticky stuff in a bowl.

'What are you doing, Mother?' Miriam asked.

Her mother jumped. She had been concentrating so hard on her work that she hadn't heard Miriam enter.

'Oh!' she exclaimed, looking up. 'I didn't hear you come in.'

Almost immediately she returned to her work, slapping the sticky black tar onto the outside of the basket. 'I'm making a boat.'

Miriam was surprised. 'A boat? That can't be a boat – it's too small.'

The smell of tar filled the tiny room as Miriam's mother continued. 'It's not supposed to be a big boat,' she said, breathing hard from the effort of tugging the basket around. 'It just needs to be big enough for the baby.'

Miriam turned around to see her little brother lying on a rug nearby. He was awake and gurgled up at his big sister. She picked him up and kissed him lightly on the cheek.

'What are you going to do?' she asked her mother. She had helped to hide the baby many times and she did so love her little brother. Suppose the Egyptian soldiers were to find him – Miriam could hardly bear to think about it!

Her mother had finished covering the outside of the basket with the tar, and she placed it in the sun to dry. She cleaned the mess off her hands before answering.

'You know your brother's too big to keep here any more,' she said, taking the baby from her daughter, 'so I've decided the only thing to do is hide him in a basket on the river and trust that God will protect him.'

Miriam stared at her mother, her eyes and mouth wide open.

'But a basket will sink, won't it?' she asked.

'Not if it's waterproofed,' her mother replied. 'That's why I've put tar all over it. The water can't get into the basket now, so it will float on the river . . .'

'But what will happen to him? Someone will find him, won't they?' Miriam asked.

'I hope not, Miriam, but I have no other choice! I've thought and thought, but this is the only solution – if he stays here any longer the Egyptian soldiers are sure to find him! We must hope that God will look after him . . .'

'I don't want to lose him!' cried Miriam. 'He's only a little baby – he's done nothing to hurt the Pharaoh!'

'I know, but it's the only way . . .' Her mother spoke quietly, and for the first time Miriam saw that there were tears in her eyes. She was trying so hard to be brave! Miriam cuddled her little brother closely as her mother lined the basket, making it soft and snug inside. The baby smiled up at his mother as she took him from his sister and lifted him into the basket. She tucked him in, and then wiped her eyes on her apron.

'I'll take the basket to the river,' Miriam murmured, putting her arm around her mother's shoulders. 'And I'll stay there and watch so I can tell you what happens.'

Her mother nodded – she was too upset to speak. Giving her son a last kiss she hurried from the room, crying.

Miriam picked up the basket and left the house. Even though it was still early and no one was about, she tried to hurry so that she wouldn't be seen. But the basket was heavy! When she reached the river she glanced around and heaved a sigh of relief – she had been so afraid of bumping into an Egyptian soldier! Tenderly she took her brother out of the basket and laid him on the bank in a safe, dry spot. Then she placed the basket on the water, testing it to make sure it floated and didn't leak.

'Mum has done a good job,' she told him, pulling the basket out of the water. 'It's quite waterproof so you'll be nice and dry inside.'

She picked him up again, and gave him a last cuddle before carefully laying him in the basket. The baby waved his little arms about as she put the basket back into the water. Once again she made sure it floated safely before leaving it hidden among the tall reeds and grasses. She wondered what would happen to her little brother!

Just then, Miriam heard voices approaching, and quickly she ran off to hide. From behind the bulrushes she watched as several young women came strolling towards the river – and stopped just where she'd been the moment before! Miriam's heart beat furiously as she recognised one of them. It was the Pharaoh's daughter! She must have come with some of her servants to bathe.

Miriam hoped desperately that her little brother had fallen asleep! But, even as she hoped, she heard a protesting cry. He didn't like his little boat!

The young women had been laughing and splashing

Egyptian Princesses. From an ancient tomb painting.

happily together, when suddenly the princess held up her hand for silence.

'What's that noise?' she asked. 'It sounds like a baby crying!'

They stood still, listening hard. In her hiding place, Miriam hardly dared breathe! Now what would happen? The little brother she was supposed to look after was about to be found by the daughter of the Pharaoh – the man who had ordered the killing of all Israelite baby boys! What could she do? What was she going to tell her mother?

Helplessly, she watched as the maids searched along the bank of the river, following the cries that became louder and louder. Meanwhile the princess waited.

'I've found it, Your Highness!' cried one of the maids. 'The sound is coming from a little basket.' She pulled away some of the long grass and dragged the basket towards the bank.

'Bring it to me!' commanded the Pharaoh's daughter, imperiously.

Two of the maids carried the basket to her, opening the lid. The princess gave a cry of surprise as she looked inside.

'It's an Israelite baby!' she exclaimed.

The baby was still crying, not liking his surroundings at all! The princess picked him up and cuddled him gently, and he stopped almost at once.

'There, there . . .' she soothed. 'Now, where did you come from?'

The baby lay in her arms and sucked at her finger.

'He's hungry, he wants to be fed.'

The maids looked blankly at one another and shrugged their shoulders, but Miriam suddenly had an idea. Creeping from her hiding place she ran towards the princess and threw herself to the ground.

'May I suggest something please, Your Highness?'

The Pharaoh's daughter was very surprised at this unexpected intrusion! However, she nodded her head slightly.

'I think I can help you . . .' Miriam began nervously.

The princess looked down at her and raised her eyebrows, wondering how this little Israelite girl could possibly be of help to the daughter of the Pharaoh!

'You can?' she asked. 'But how?'

Miriam took a deep breath, but then she hesitated . . . her idea had seemed simple when she'd first thought of it, but now, kneeling in front of the princess, she wasn't so sure! The princess waited patiently.

'Your Highness, I know an Israelite woman who has just lost her child,' Miriam told her truthfully. 'She would be able to feed this baby for you.'

The princess thought for a moment and then smiled. 'Good! Go and find this woman, and bring her to me.'

Miriam backed away, bowing clumsily. Then she turned, and ran as fast as she could back to her home.

'Mum! Mum!,' she shouted as she ran into the house, panting. 'Come here, quickly!'

Her mother rushed to meet her, her face pale with worry.

'What's wrong? What's happened! It's the baby isn't, it?' she gasped.

'The Pharaoh's daughter has found him!' Miriam replied.

'Oh no!' Her mother put her hand over her mouth, cutting off her cry of horror. Her dear little son! What would the princess do with him?

'No – you don't understand . . .' continued Miriam, still out of breath from her run. 'He's quite safe! She wants me to find a woman to look after him! But we must hurry in case she changes her mind.'

'What? But I don't . . .' But Miriam didn't have time to waste! She grabbed her mother by the hand and pulled her out of the house. As they hurried back to the river, she explained everything to her.

Miriam was worried that the princess might have decided not to wait for her and gone home – but she was still there when they returned, fussing over the baby and talking to him. Breathlessly, she pulled her mother towards the princess, bowing deeply, her heart pounding.

'This is the woman I told you about, Your Highness.'

The princess turned to the older woman.

'This girl says you've just lost a baby.'

The mother nodded. 'My baby is no longer with me,' she replied truthfully, gazing longingly at her son in the princess's arms.

'I have just found this baby, and I want you to look after him for me,' commanded the princess. 'Can you do it? You will be well paid.'

'I will do as you ask . . .' she murmured, finding it difficult to believe what she heard. Her heart was bursting with excitement.

'The baby is now my son,' said the princess. 'I will call him Moses, because I pulled him out of the water.'

She gave him to Miriam's mother who cradled him lovingly in her arms.

'Be sure to look after him well,' she said, 'Don't worry about the soldiers. They will be ordered to stay away from your home, and my servants will make sure that my son has everything he needs.'

'Yes, Your Highness. Thank you!'

Miriam and her mother bowed and hurried home. They didn't speak because they were still stunned and shocked by what had just taken place!

A nomadic tribe travelling with their animals and possessions.

But it must be true, thought Miriam, for there, in her mother's arms, was the precious baby. Her brother was coming home with them again, but this time they knew he couldn't be harmed. He was safe under the orders of the Pharaoh's own daughter!

When he was old enough, Moses moved into the Pharaoh's palace, where he grew into a fine young man. But as time went on, he came to feel more and more that he was an Israelite, and not an Egyptian.

Miriam stayed at home to help her mother, who by now had another baby to care for. She had named him Aaron, and as the Pharaoh had stopped killing the Israelite boys soon after Moses had been rescued, her new baby was quite safe. The Israelites, however, were still slaves. One day God spoke to Moses. He asked him to lead his people to freedom, in a land of their own.

Time and time again, Moses asked the Pharaoh to allow the Israelites to leave Egypt, but every time the Pharaoh refused. He needed thousands of slaves to build his great cities and temples, and to work for the Egyptians in their houses and fields. He didn't want the Israelites to become more powerful than their masters – but neither did he want to lose them altogether!

So God sent many pests and sicknesses to the land, until the Pharaoh eventually sent for Moses again.

'Alright! The Israelite people can leave Egypt!' he shouted at him. 'And the sooner the better!'

So Moses, Miriam and Aaron led the thousands of Israelites out of Egypt. It was an enormous job, with everyone wanting to take all their animals and possessions with them. It took a great deal of time and organisation!

From an Egyptian wall painting.

The carved lid of Ramesses II's coffin shows him as Osiris, the Egyptian god of the dead.

Not long after they had left however, the Pharaoh changed his mind again.

'I must be mad!' he told himself. 'I can't possibly run my country without all my slaves! I must get them back at once!'

He summoned his army officers to him at the palace.

'Get your soldiers after those Israelites immediately!' he roared. 'How dare they defy the King of Egypt!'

The soldiers set off – in their chariots and on foot – determined to overtake the escaping Israelites as quickly as possible. It wasn't until they neared the Red Sea that they caught sight of them.

'We've got them now!' cried the Egyptian general. 'They're trapped against the sea, they can't escape. It's too dark to do any more tonight, we'll camp here and round them up in the morning.'

The soldiers didn't sleep well that night. A strong easterly wind that whistled through the camp. In the horse lines the grooms struggled to keep order, as their charges whinnied nervously. The blown sand got everywhere – into their clothes, into their eyes, and even into their breakfasts!

They rose before dawn and set off to finish the job. It should be easy – the Israelites couldn't have gone far. Fancy travelling with all that luggage. How could they expect to escape from the Pharaoh!

But as they approached the coast, the Egyptians were stopped in their tracks. The Israelites had vanished, and what was more – so had the sea!

The general was the first to recover from the surprise. Looking into the distance he could see the end of the Israelite column as it approached the far shore.

'After them!' he shouted, waving his sword above his head. 'They mustn't escape!'

Ramesses II in his chariot. He is believed by many scholars to have been the pharaoh at the time of the Exodus.

With drums and trumpets sounding the horses thundered forward. The air rang with the sound of war cries as the furious army advanced. The charioteers led the charge, the multi coloured plumes on their horses heads billowing in the wind, the wheels bouncing over the rocky shore. Running furiously, their spears glistening in the dawn sun, the foot soldiers streamed behind them, determined not to miss the fun.

This was something new – they had never charged into the sea before! They laughed and joked as they encouraged each other onwards.

However, the further they went the slower they seemed to be travelling. The chariots were slowing – their wheels sinking into the ground. Eventually they came to a halt, completely bogged down, with mud up to their axles. The horses were exhausted and their legs were being sucked into the mire. No matter how much the riders and drivers urged them, they could move no further. Panic started to set in.

Worse was to come! Now that they were stuck fast, the sea began pouring back towards them! The general was terrified.

He had promised Pharaoh that he'd bring the Israelites back. Not only had he failed to catch them, but he had led his own troops to a watery grave!

Turning to look back, Miriam saw that the water had returned and there was now no sign of the passage that God had opened for them. The Israelites had escaped – they had all passed safely across!

Moses led his people into the desert, where they were to stay for many years. God spoke to the Israelites through his prophets – Moses, Miriam and Aaron, teaching them to live in the way he wanted.

Moses, the little boy that Miriam had saved from the Egyptians, had led the Israelites from slavery to freedom. But it was to be other prophets and leaders that were to lead them into the Promised Land . . .

Winning the battle

The people of Israel had forgotten all about God! They had been in the Promised Land for many years, but no longer lived the way they had been shown after their escape from Egypt. Indeed, they didn't even worship God any more because they felt that they could manage on their own!

Then the time came when an enemy conquered the Israelites. King Jabin and his Canaanite army had fought against them and won, and for the next twenty years the people of Israel were subjected to his cruelty and violence. The Israelites were no match for the iron chariots of Jabin's powerful army. As they suffered they started to remember God, and begged him to help them again.

Hearing their cries, God spoke to Deborah; a Judge – one of the leaders of Israel. She didn't have an office in a large building but sat under a palm tree in the shade. Every day people would come to her with all sorts of problems, and Deborah, a very wise prophet, would give them her advice.

One day, Deborah sent for Barak, from the tribe of Issachar.

'I have had a message from God,' she told him as they sat together under the tree.

Barak nodded politely, and waited to see what else she had to say.

'You are to take ten thousand men to Mount Tabor,' Deborah continued. 'Sisera will lead Jabin's army there – and you will fight against him!'

Barak was speechless. He knew that Sisera commanded an army of thousands of soldiers and nine hundred powerful iron chariots! What chance did he have against the mighty Canaanites?

'God . . . wants me to fight . . . against Sisera?' he stammered.

'That's right,' Deborah replied.

'But Sisera has so much experience and his army is very well trained. What can we do against such a force?'

'He may well have all these men,' answered Deborah, 'but God has told me you will have the victory – he has promised that you will win.'

Many questions raced through Barak's mind. Why had he been chosen? Was Deborah speaking the truth? What if she were mistaken? Meanwhile Deborah sat quietly watching the world go by. She knew what Barak was thinking; it was a decision that only he could make.

After some minutes Barak spoke.

'I'll go,' he said slowly, 'but only if you come with me. If you won't go neither will I.'

'All right,' Deborah said, nodding her head. 'I'll go too, but I must warn you. Although you will win the battle you won't get the credit for defeating Sisera because he will be handed over to a woman.'

Now Barak was more confused. Handed over to a woman – whatever did Deborah mean? He shook his head in puzzlement. All he knew was that he had agreed to fight a battle – and that first he had to find an army. This could be a problem!

They set off together, to visit the tribes of Zebulun and Naphtali, asking the men to join them in the fight against Sisera. Many were keen to go – this was the chance they had been waiting for! Now they could get rid of Sisera and the evil Jabin. Some of the men, however, weren't so sure:

'Who will look after our sheep while we're away?'

'What match are we for Sisera's chariots?'

'I think we'll be safer staying here!'

But in the end, Barak and Deborah raised an army of ten thousand men . . .

A Canaanite Prince accepts gifts and slaves from a conquered foe. He appears again on the right riding in his iron chariot. From a 3000 year old ivory plaque.

Sisera, meanwhile, was resting in his tent, waiting for his dinner to be served. He looked up when he heard someone being challenged by his bodyguards.

'Well! Come in!' demanded Sisera. 'Have you got my meal?'

'I haven't, Sir . . .' quaked the nervous soldier.

'What are you doing here then?' roared the general.

'Sorry to interrupt, Sir, but we have just heard. There's an Israelite called Barak . . .'

'Well what about him? This had better be important . . .' snarled Sisera.

'They say he's collecting together an Israelite army.'

'Well, what if he is? No matter how many men he has we will grind them into the dust. We'll show these Israelites that they must respect the power of King Jabin the Invincible!' Sisera sat up, and rearranged his cushions more comfortably, before continuing.

'How many of this rabble have the courage to meet us on the field of battle?'

'About ten thousand, Sir,' the soldier replied.

'And what about horses and chariots?'

'None to match ours, Sir.'

Sisera laughed. 'Ten thousand Israelite men? Is that all?' He laughed louder. 'Do you call that an army?'

The soldier stood up straighter, hardly daring to move. 'No, Sir.'

'And what is this man . . . what did you say his name was?'

'Barak, Sir,' replied the soldier.

'Ah yes, Barak,' nodded Sisera. 'And what is this Barak doing with his so-called army?'

'I understand he is heading towards Mount Tabor, Sir.'

'Mount Tabor?' said Sisera slowly. 'Why, he's just like the rest – skulking up in the hills!'

Crossing the tent, he drew back the curtain covering the door. Before them in all directions stretched Jabin's army, the mid-day sun shimmering on a sea of helmets, swords and shields.

'That,' he said, 'is an army!'

He returned to the shade of his headquarters, and shouted for his commanders.

'Prepare to leave! We will massacre the Israelites at the River Kishon!'

Still the soldier hesitated.

'There . . . there is something else, sir,' he stammered.

'Yes?' Sisera raised one eyebrow.

'Barak doesn't lead this army alone. There is someone else with him – a woman.'

'A woman!' Sisera sneered. 'Barak dares to come and fight a battle against me and commands his army with a woman!'

The soldier was silent. He wished he hadn't mentioned it.

'I fear no man,' said Sisera coldly, 'much less do I fear a woman!' Then an ugly smile crossed his face and he laughed. 'A woman! This battle will be even easier than I first thought. Let us go to the river . . .'

As the officers and men rushed around, preparing to depart, Sisera turned back to the messenger.

'It's obvious – no one could defeat such a powerful army!'

Deborah and Barak were camped on Mount Tabor with their army, preparing for the battle. Looking up into the sky, Deborah saw huge black clouds rolling towards them. There was going to be a great storm very soon. She stood up and signalled that it was time to leave.

'Go!' she ordered. 'The time has come for you to fight and for God to lead you to victory over Sisera!'

Deborah watched Barak's army charging down the steep hillside towards the unsuspecting Canaanites. As the Israelites approached the river, the storm broke, and torrents of rain poured from the sky. Deborah's timing was perfect. Sisera's men were so busy trying to quieten their horses and find shelter from the rain that they were completely surprised by Barak's attack.

The invincible army was thrown into total confusion! Foot soldiers were shouting and trying to find their weapons. Riderless horses whinnied as they galloped through the storm. Chariots raced round and round in circles, colliding with each other, their drivers desperate to escape. The ground, churned up by wheels and hooves, was soon a sea of mud, and the heavy iron chariots became hopelessly bogged down. The torrential rain made it impossible for the soldiers to see where they were going.

Sisera watched the confusion and saw that the impossible was happening. His men had been taken completely by surprise and didn't know where to go or what to do! Their mighty chariots, so strong and powerful, were useless! His army was doomed.

*A Canaanite raises his hand in salute.
From an ancient bronze plaque.*

Sisera's bravery vanished and he now felt very frightened. He slowed his chariot and jumped to the ground, stumbling as he fell. Picking himself up, his sodden clothes caked in mud, he began to run as fast as he could away from the battle and his army.

No one saw him leave. His own men were trying to run in the opposite direction, away from the Israelites who were slaughtering every enemy soldier they could lay their hands on. Sisera could see that not one of his mighty army would survive that dreadful day.

Barak stood on the field, amazed by what his army had done. His thoughts were interrupted by the approach of one of his friends.

'We've checked the dead, Barak, but we can't find Sisera. He isn't amongst them.'

'He must be,' said Barak angrily. 'Unless . . .' A thought suddenly came to him. 'Perhaps he ran away and left his men to die!'

Barak turned and walked across the battlefield. He swore that he wouldn't rest until he found him. Only when Sisera was dead would he feel that he'd really won the battle.

Sisera meanwhile had run away as fast as he could. He didn't know where he was going, he just knew he had to put as much distance as possible between himself and the battlefield! He kept going until the sounds of fighting had been left far behind. Then he looked back, and when he was sure that he wasn't being followed, he finally threw himself panting to the ground.

It wasn't raining any more but Sisera's muddy clothes were soaked and stuck to his skin. He staggered on – he wasn't used to all this walking, he normally travelled everywhere in his chariot. Eventually he saw some tents in the distance. He now realised where he was! These were the tents of Heber the Kenite – and Heber was at peace with King Jabin.

'The gods be praised!' Sisera muttered to himself. 'These people will provided me with everything I want.'

He checked behind him cautiously before he entered the camp, making absolutely sure that he hadn't been followed. No – there wasn't a soul in sight. He had escaped from those terrible Israelites at last!

He was about to call out and announce his arrival when the flap of a tent opened and a woman stepped out to meet him. Sisera recognised her at once. She was Jael, the wife of Heber.

'Why, Sisera!' she smiled, 'What a surprise! Are you here all alone?'

Sisera nodded. 'Is your husband at home?'

'No – no, he's not here at the moment,' she answered. 'I'm the only one around! Oh dear, did you come all this way to see him?'

'Yes!' Sisera snapped sharply. He was feeling uncomfortable in his damp, torn clothes and he didn't want to answer any questions! The woman looked Sisera up and down, noting his filthy tunic and mud-smeared face.

'You look as if you need to get cleaned up,' she continued. 'Why don't you come in – you'll be much more comfortable.' Seeing him hesitate she added: 'It's alright – I won't let anybody know you're here.'

Sisera marched straight into the tent.

'I'd like a drink,' he ordered. 'I've come a long way.'

She pointed to a curtain on the other side of the tent.

'You hide behind there and no one will see you,' she said. 'I'll get you a drink. You do look thirsty.'

Jael opened a leather bag and gave him a long drink of milk which he gulped down.

'Ah – that was good,' he said, handing the bag back to her. 'I feel much better after that!'

Now that his thirst had been quenched, Sisera realised that he was exhausted. It had been a long day – he'd been up early and had run a long way from where the battle had taken place. He lay down in his hiding place behind the curtain.

'I feel very tired,' he told Jael. 'I think I'll lie here for a few minutes and rest. I want you to keep watch for me. If anyone comes along asking if I'm here, you haven't seen me.'

Jael smiled her strange smile. 'Don't worry — I'll look after you,' she promised. 'There's no reason to be afraid . . .'

Within a few minutes, Sisera was fast asleep. As soon as Jael heard him snoring regularly, she crept quietly towards him and lifted the curtain. The great Sisera lay defenceless at her feet.

From beneath the folds of her cloak, Jael now withdrew a tent-peg and a heavy wooden mallet. She crept right up to the unsuspecting Sisera and placed the pointed end of the peg against his head, just beside his ear.

'There is nothing to fear here, Sisera . . .' she whispered as she raised the mallet high in the air '. . . nothing to fear at all! After all, I am only a woman!'

Some hours later Barak entered the camp searching for his enemy. He too was tired, thirsty and furious that Sisera had given him the slip. Jael came out of her tent as he approached.

'I am looking for Sisera, the leader of Jabin's army,' Barak called to her. 'Have you seen him?'

Without a word Jael beckoned him closer. She pointed inside the tent.

'Come in — I'll show you the man you're looking for,' she said.

He followed her into the tent and gasped as she pulled the curtain aside. There on the ground at his feet lay Sisera's dead body. As he stared at it, Barak remembered what Deborah had said under the palm tree.

'You will win the battle but a woman will kill Sisera.'

Deborah had been right in all she had said.

Barak left the camp to return to his victorious army. Everyone was celebrating, thanking God for giving them the great triumph he had promised. Barak knew now that it would only be a short time before the Israelites defeated King Jabin himself and were free again!

A binding love

It was very hot! The sun baked the ground dry, all day and every day. Even in the shade it was almost unbearable. Sitting with her back to the trunk of a tree, Naomi was glad of what little shade it gave. She had had a long day and was taking a well deserved rest before heading home.

She had seen it all before! Many years ago in Israel there had been a terrible drought which had lasted so long that she had been forced to leave her home. As a result her family had arrived in the neighbouring country of Moab – they had been lured by stories of plentiful food and rain.

Over the years her sons, Mahlon and Chilion, had grown up and become a part of the community. But shortly before they were to marry – to two local girls, Orpah and Ruth – Naomi's husband had died. Ten years later she was to suffer another tragedy, for both her beloved sons were to die within a short time of one another.

As she sat under the tree Naomi reflected on how her life had changed. Now she was alone, with her daughters-in-law, in a foreign land. They had no men to look after them, and life was becoming hard. What was she to do and how were they to live? All her relatives lived in Israel – which was still in the grip of famine – so they wouldn't be able to help!

Her thoughts were interrupted by the sound of voices. Opening her eyes she saw some travellers coming towards her. She didn't feel like talking to anyone today, so she closed her eyes again, pretending to be asleep.

The group walked by, quite close to Naomi, but they didn't even bother to look at her. They were too busy talking amongst themselves to notice a woman lying asleep under a tree!

'My brother, Reuben, leaves for Israel tomorrow,' said one voice.

'Israel!' exclaimed another, surprised. 'Why does he want to go there?'

'There's still a famine, isn't there?

'There was a famine,' replied the first, 'but it's over now. There have been good rains and the crops are thick and high. Reuben says . . .'

The group walked on and Naomi heard no more. But she had heard enough! As she opened her eyes, her brain was racing.

The famine was over! If there was plenty to eat she could return to her home. Her relatives would welcome her back! But what about Ruth and Orpah? Moab was their country and their families lived here. For a long time she sat there, wondering what to do. She didn't want to say goodbye to them for she loved both girls dearly, but it wasn't fair for her to ask them to go to Israel with her. They must remain here in Moab and she would return alone.

Having decided, Naomi stood up, brushing the dust from her clothes and set off for home, making her plans as she walked.

'Ruth! . . . Orpah!'

The two young women ran out of the house when they heard Naomi's call.

'What's wrong?' Orpah enquired, her face full of concern.

Naomi shook her head. 'Nothing's wrong, Orpah,' she reassured the worried girl. 'But I have been thinking hard this afternoon and I've decided that I must return to Israel . . .'

'But the famine . . .' Ruth butted in.

'There isn't a famine any more,' Naomi explained. 'I've just heard some people talking about it. They said there is plenty of food there now.'

'Are you really sure?' Orpah enquired. 'People do tell all kinds of stories.'

Naomi nodded her head. 'I'm sure,' she replied.

'Well then,' Ruth exclaimed, heading back to the house. 'What are we waiting for? Let's start packing our bags . . .'

Naomi looked at her daughter-in-law with sad eyes. 'We aren't leaving, Ruth,' she said. 'I am returning to Israel alone. You and Orpah must stay here.'

'But we can't do that!' cried Ruth. 'We love you very much – we want to stay with you!'

'And I love you both as well . . .' Naomi replied, clasping their hands. 'But it isn't right for you to come with me. Your families are here, so you should stay with them.'

Tears appeared in Naomi's eyes and Orpah began to cry aloud. She hugged Naomi, kissing her on both cheeks.

'I don't want to stay here. You know I want to go with you
. . . but I'll do as you ask.'

Orpah hurried away to pack her few belongings and return
to her own family.

Tears were streaming down Ruth's cheeks too, but she
held onto her mother-in-law's hand.

'Don't make me go away,' she pleaded.

Naomi stared down at the ground, trying to hide her own
tears.

'You must go home too! Israel is my country and it
wouldn't be fair to take you there. I will be all right on my
own.'

Ruth's voice changed as she came to a decision. 'No!' she
said stubbornly. 'I'm going with you. Nothing will change
my mind!'

Naomi wiped her eyes and gazed at Ruth. She knew that
once this young woman had made up her mind, nothing
would change it!

'All right, then. Let's prepare for our journey!'

The two women travelled on foot to Bethlehem, carrying
the few possessions they owned. It had been a long time
since Naomi had left for Moab with her family, but many of

the townspeople recognised her and were pleased to see her again.

'Naomi! Is that really you?' called one of her old neighbours. 'What a long time you've been away!' Others joined him, and soon the two women were surrounded by welcoming faces.

'It has been a long time,' Naomi told them. 'I left with plenty but now I have very little – my husband and sons are dead.'

Her old friends murmered sympathetically.

'And who is this?' someone asked her, pointing to Ruth.

'This is Ruth, Mahlon's widow. She has come to live with me . . .'

The two women found somewhere to stay, but after a few days Ruth realised that their meagre savings were disappearing fast. Soon they would have no more food . . .

'I'm going out into the fields today.' she told her mother-in-law the next morning, as she arranged her head-dress carefully against the glaring sun.

'The harvest has just begun – I saw some workers out in the fields yesterday – and I may be able to collect the stalks of barley they miss with their sickles . . .'

Naomi waved goodbye and closed the door, knowing that Ruth would do her best to find them something to eat.

Ruth hurried from the house to the field where she had seen the workers the day before. Even though it was still early morning, they were already hard at work gathering the golden grain. Moving slowly up and down the fields, they cut down the tall barley stalks before tying them up into sheaves. Sometimes a few stalks would fall onto the ground and these they left – the harvesters weren't allowed to pick them up again. These 'gleanings' were for the poor and needy of the villages who followed the reapers around the fields picking up the leftovers.

Ruth entered the field and joined the other gleaners. It was hard work. Her back ached from constantly bending over and her hands became sore and rough from gathering the sharp stalks. The sun blazed down on her head and she was soon thirsty and hot, but she didn't stop working. She knew she had to collect enough barley for Naomi to grind into flour, and what she had so far was not sufficient.

At midday, the workers stopped for lunch, so Ruth felt that

she too had earned a break. She groaned a little as she stood up, for her back was aching – she wasn't used to this sort of work! There was a large tree growing on one side of the field and Ruth decided this would be the best place to rest. She hadn't brought any lunch with her, but she would, she decided, sit in the shade and perhaps have a short nap.

Just as Ruth was settling down under the tree, the landowner, a rich man called Boaz, came strolling into the field. He had decided to come and see how the harvest was progressing, and now he called out greetings to his workers who were enjoying their rest. He glanced over the field and nodded as the foreman showed him what work had been

Harvesters drinking from a bottle made from the skin of an animal.

done that morning. Then he noticed Ruth lying in the shade.

'Who is that young woman over there?' he asked, pointing in her direction.

The foreman shaded his eyes against the sun.

'Oh, that's the girl who came back from Moab with Naomi,' he answered. 'She arrived here early this morning and asked if she could follow the workers. She has been gleaning ever since. I've been watching her and she's only now gone to sit down to have a rest.'

Boaz nodded to his foreman and wandered across his field to the tree where Ruth was sitting. As he approached, she jumped to her feet, recognizing him as the land-owner.

'Oh sir, I did ask the man in charge if I could follow the workers,' she exclaimed nervously. 'And he said it was all right! I hope I haven't done anything wrong!'

Boaz held up his hand to quieten her. 'No, no,' he said smiling. 'You haven't done anything wrong. And I know you've been working hard this morning, so sit down and rest. I want to talk to you.'

Ruth, still unsure, sat down slowly. Boaz sat beside her in the shade.

'First,' he said. 'Tell me your name.'

'Ruth,' she replied.

'All right Ruth, listen to me. Stay in this field to collect your grain. You will be quite safe if you stay near the other women who are also picking up stalks.'

Ruth nodded. She had seen several other women in the field that morning and had felt safe in their company.

'Picking up grain is thirsty work,' Boaz continued. 'Whenever you want a drink just go to the water jars and drink from them.'

He pointed to the line of jars that had been placed in the field for the workers to use.

Ruth looked up at him in surprise. 'Why are you being so kind to me?' she asked. 'You don't know me, and I don't even come from your country.'

Boaz smiled at her. 'I've heard how you left your own family and country to come here with your mother-in-law. And I've also heard from my foreman how hard you've worked this morning. I feel you deserve some kindness shown to you as well. May God bless you.'

She blushed at his kind words. 'Thank you sir,' she replied. 'You are very kind.'

'You must be hungry and thirsty now,' he said, standing up. 'Have you brought anything to eat?' Ruth shook her head.

'Then you must come and join us in our meal,' he said, helping her to her feet.

Leaving her precious bundle of barley under the tree, she followed him back to where the workers were eating their meal. Boaz shared his food with her and gave her a drink. She was hungry after working for so long, and the water was cool and refreshing. Ruth ate until she had had enough and the food that was left over she wrapped carefully to take home for Naomi. Thanking Boaz again for his kindness, she returned to her work.

When she was too far away to hear, Boaz called his workers together

'I want you to let that young woman have as much grain as possible,' he ordered. 'Miss some stalks or simply pull some barley from your bundles and leave it lying on the ground for her to pick up. It doesn't matter how you do it as long as she collects plenty of grain.'

As Boaz left the field, the workers returned to their job, discussing his orders amongst themselves. They did as they were told – and Ruth suddenly found she had more than enough grain to collect! She worked all afternoon and as evening approached she beat out all the grain from the heads of the stalks and took it home to Naomi. She also carried home the food she'd saved from her meal with Boaz.

Naomi welcomed her at the door, glad that Ruth had come home. She had been lonely by herself.

'Oh Ruth, dear,' she said. 'What a long day you've had! Come in, sit down and tell me what happened.'

Ruth placed the package of grain and food on the table, smiling. Then she sat down, tenderly rubbing her feet with her sore, rough hands. Her back ached but she was pleased with her day's work.

Naomi opened the cloth and saw all the grain inside.

'Ruth!' she cried, her eyes wide with astonishment. 'How did you find so much barley? Whose field have you been working in?'

'It belongs to a man called Boaz,' Ruth smiled. 'Look, he gave me some food to eat as well! I've kept some for you . . .'

She began to unwrap the parcel of food but Naomi wasn't paying any attention.

'Boaz?' she asked. 'Boaz? Of all the fields around here, you chose to work in Boaz's field?'

Ruth stared at her in surprise. 'Do you know him? Is anything wrong?'

Naomi smiled. 'Nothing is wrong, child,' she said. 'And yes, I know Boaz! He is a close relative of ours, and I'm sure he'll look after us.'

Now Ruth understood why Boaz had been so kind to her.

He had known who she was all the time but hadn't told her!

'He suggested I go to that field every day until the harvest has finished,' she told Naomi.

'That is most kind of him,' her mother-in-law agreed as she began to eat the food Ruth had brought home. 'God has certainly blessed us today, my child!'

All through the harvest Ruth worked in Boaz's fields, picking first the barley and then the wheat. It was always hot, thirsty work and she was tired out by evening, but she was happy and the two women were never hungry. Boaz often came to the field and he and Ruth would share a meal or just sit and talk under a tree.

Eventually, Ruth and Boaz were married. They lived very happily together, and their son, Obed, grew up to be the father of Jesse, who in turn was the father of the great King David. Ruth, the poor widow from a foreign land, would be remembered as the great-grandmother of Israel's most famous king!

God answers prayer

Elkanah was a farmer who lived with his wife, Hannah, in the hills of Israel. He was a good farmer and had many animals and crops to care for. Hannah loved her husband very much. She would have been very happy except for one thing – she didn't have any children.

Every year, the couple would travel to the nearby town of Shiloh, where they'd stay for several days. Here they would worship in the Tabernacle – the House of God where the Covenent Box was kept.

One year, as they began their journey, Hannah was very quiet. Even when they'd arrived in Shiloh she wouldn't talk to Elkanah, but spent much of the time on her own crying. To make matters worse she wouldn't eat, and Elkanah was afraid that she would become ill.

'Hannah, are you ready?' Elkanah called to her one morning shortly after they'd arrived at Shiloh. 'It's time for us to visit the Tabernacle.'

Hannah entered the room slowly. Elkanah couldn't see her face, but he heard a small sniff.

'Have you been crying again?' he asked quietly.

She shook her head, but he went up to her and lifted her chin with his finger. Her eyes were red and swollen.

'Oh, Hannah – you have!'

She wiped her eyes, blew her nose and dropped her head again.

'What's wrong, my wife? You've been crying ever since we arrived here.'

Hannah sniffed again and glanced up at him.

'You know what's wrong,' she whispered. 'I want a baby so much . . .'

Once again the tears began to fall down her cheeks. Elkanah put his arm around her shoulders and squeezed her gently.

'You have me,' he said lovingly.

'Oh, Elkanah, I know!' Hannah answered. 'And I love you as well! But it's not the same . . . you don't know what it's like when the other women talk about their babies and children! I have to listen to them and it hurts. It's not fair!'

'I know . . . I know.'

Elkanah felt helpless. He had seen Hannah upset before and knew how sad she was, but what could he say? He held her close until her sobbing stopped and she wiped her eyes again.

'There now,' he said, 'crying isn't going to help, is it? Let's have something to eat before we go to the Tabernacle . . .'

Again Hannah shook her head. 'I can't eat,' she said. 'I'm too upset. Anyway . . . I'm not hungry.'

He stepped back, looking at her, a worried expression on his face. Her cheeks, streaked with tears, were thin and pale.

'But you must eat something,' he insisted. 'You haven't eaten anything for days!'

Still she shook her head and Elkanah gave in.

'Well, let's go and worship. Perhaps when we come back you'll feel better and eat something.'

'I doubt it,' she replied.

When they arrived at the Tabernacle, Hannah went inside and began to pray. As she did so, all the unhappiness poured out of her and she began to cry again, bitterly. She was so unhappy! If only she had a child of her own, she thought, then everything would be alright!

'Oh Lord, please give me a baby!' she prayed. 'You know I have wanted a son for so long. I promise I will give him back to you, for his whole life, if you'll only answer my prayer!'

Again and again she prayed, repeating the words over and over in her head. Her lips moved but no sound came. The tears still trickled down her cheeks. She stayed there for a long time asking God to give her a son. Never in her life had she prayed so hard!

Eli, the priest in charge of the Tabernacle, sat near the door. He had seen many people come and go as they offered their prayers to God – but as he watched Hannah a frown darkened his face.

'I do believe that woman's drunk,' he thought to himself. He looked harder, hardly able to credit what he could see! Hannah's body swayed to and fro, and her mouth spoke words no one could hear. He hoped that she'd leave before anyone else came in and saw her. But she didn't. She stayed where she was with her eyes tightly closed.

At last Eli stood up and strode over to her.

'Woman!' he snorted. 'You should be ashamed of yourself coming in here like this!'

Hannah jumped slightly as he spoke. She had been concentrating so hard on her prayer she hadn't heard him approach, and his voice had frightened her. She opened her eyes and spun around to face him.

'I'm sorry,' she stammered. 'You startled me! What did you say?'

Eli looked at her sternly. 'This is the House of the Lord!' he told her. 'How dare you come in here when you are drunk! Go away at once and sober up!'

Hannah stared at him, trying to understand what he meant.

' I'm sorry, I don't know what you're talking about.' Then she flushed. 'I . . . I'm not drunk.'

'Of course you are!' replied the priest scornfully. 'I've been watching you for quite a long time. You've been muttering away to yourself and swaying so much it's obvious you can hardly stand upright!'

In spite of herself, Hannah smiled. She had no idea what she had looked like.

'I'm not drunk – really I'm not!' she assured him. 'I was just praying very hard. I've been so sad lately, and I decided to tell God all my troubles and ask for help.'

'Oh dear – I'm so sorry!' Eli now looked very embarrassed. 'I shouldn't have thought so badly of you! I didn't realise you were praying . . .'

'I was only praying like that because I was so upset,' Hannah explained. 'I was asking God for something I want desperately.'

'Then may the Lord give you what you've asked for,' smiled Eli, placing his hand on her head. 'Now, go in peace and trust that God will answer your prayer.'

As Hannah made her way out, Eli shook his head shamefacedly. What a terrible mistake he had made! He returned to his seat by the door and prayed that she would be granted what she wanted so much . . .

Hannah met Elkanah outside, and they walked back to the house together. Elkanah glanced sideways at his wife, puzzled. Earlier, she had walked with one foot dragging sadly behind the other, but now she was tripping lightly with a spring in her step! He didn't say anything but he knew she was no longer unhappy. Something had happened to her.

'I'll be glad to get back,' she informed him, breaking the silence. 'I'm really hungry!'

'Hungry?' he exclaimed, astonished. 'A few hours ago you wouldn't eat anything! Something's happened to you Hannah – I wish you'd tell me what it was!'

'Oh, I feel as if a great load has been taken from my shoulders,' she laughed. 'I prayed harder today than I have ever done in my life! I asked God for a son – and I feel sure that my prayer will be answered!'

Her husband smiled at her. 'Well, I'm pleased that you're happy again,' he said. 'I told you that worrying wouldn't help, didn't I?'

Hannah nodded, smiling. From the moment she had finished praying she had felt calm and peaceful, confident that God had heard her prayers and was going to answer them . . .

Hannah was right. A little less than a year later she gave birth to a beautiful baby son.

'I'm going to call him Samuel,' she told Elkanah happily. 'It means "I asked the Lord for him." '

They were both thrilled with their little boy, knowing he was a special gift from God. Next year, when the time came for them to go to Shiloh again, Hannah decided to remain at home.

'Samuel isn't old enough to travel yet,' she decided. 'You go to Shiloh and I'll stay at home with him.'

'You do whatever you think is best, dear,' her husband replied, and prepared to make the journey without her.

'I haven't forgotten my promise,' she added, as she waved goodbye. 'I said that I would give my son to God as a gift, and as soon as he's old enough, I will.'

Hannah kept her promise. When Samuel was still a very little boy, she took him to Shiloh and went in search of Eli, the priest. She found him sitting in his usual place, and when he saw her he rose to his feet.

'Excuse me, sir,' she ventured, holding her son's hand tightly, uncertain how to begin. Eli waited. He had seen this woman before, but couldn't remember where.

'I wonder if you remember me?' she continued. 'I am the woman you saw praying here in the Tabernacle – you thought I was drunk!'

Eli suddenly smiled as he recognised her. 'How could I forget?' he said. 'I've never felt so embarrassed! You were praying hard, weren't you?'

Hannah relaxed a little and smiled. 'That's right,' she answered. 'I was praying for something I desperately wanted – a child . . . a son.' She moved Samuel forward a little. 'As you can see, God has answered my prayer.'

The priest glanced down at the boy and placed his wrinkled hand on Samuel's shoulder.

'He is a fine boy and God has richly blessed you,' he said.

Hannah took a deep breath. It was now time to carry out her promise.

'I vowed that if God answered my prayer I would give my son back to the Lord. Samuel belongs to God as long as he lives.'

Eli glanced from the boy to his mother, not sure if he understood what she meant.

'Do you mean you want your son to remain here, with me?' he asked slowly.

'That's right,' Hannah replied. 'God answered my prayer and I must keep my promise. My son belongs to God, and I'm asking you to look after him for me!'

Tears filled the old man's eyes. He knew that this woman really meant what she said, but he could also see how difficult it was for her to give away the precious son that she had prayed so hard for. .

'I'll take your son and care for him,' he said, taking Samuel's hand. 'God bless you for your gift. Shall we go and worship and give thanks together?'

The little group of three – the priest, the young boy and his mother worshipped God, presenting Samuel to the Lord's service. When they had finished, Hannah gave her son a last hug and left him with Eli, promising to see him every year when she and Elkanah returned to Shiloh.

The following year when Hannah and Elkanah returned to Shiloh, she brought a present for Samuel. The year had passed slowly for Hannah and, as she watched her son eagerly open the parcel, she noticed how much he had grown.

'It's a robe!' cried Samuel, holding it up.

'I made it specially for you,' his mother smiled proudly. 'I'll make you a new one every year . . .'

Samuel hugged his mother. 'I'm going to put it on right now!' he shouted excitedly as he ran off. Less than a minute later he returned, Eli and Elkanah walking beside him. The robe was not on straight, but it was a perfect fit, and Samuel was proudly showing it to the priest.

'That's just what you need!' agreed Eli, smiling. He turned to Samuel's parents. 'He is growing fast, isn't he? How clever of you to make sure it was just the right size!'

Playfully he ruffled the boy's hair. Samuel laughed and then ran off to do some jobs for Eli. The priest watched him go.

'May God bless you for giving Samuel to us,' he said as he turned back to Hannah and Elkanah. 'He is a fine boy! He learns so quickly, and serves God well. I hope you have many more children just like him.'

Hannah felt sad as once again they left to return home, but she didn't forget to thank God for her precious son.

As the years passed, Samuel studied God's word and learned from Eli. He looked forward to seeing his parents every year – and his mother never forgot to bring him a new robe!

Samuel grew up to be a great Judge of Israel, specially called by God. He was God's servant for the whole of his life, just as Hannah had promised he would be.

'I haven't any bread!'

Ahab had been king of Israel for many years, but in all that time he hadn't worshipped God. Instead, he'd put up large statues of other gods, and built temples where he could worship them. Seeing this, God at last became angry and decided to punish Ahab by sending a drought to his country.

Now, not far away there lived a man called Elijah who was a prophet, a messenger of God. One night, in a dream, God told Elijah to go to King Ahab and give him a warning. So several days later Elijah stood before the king in his magnificent palace.

'I have a message for you from God,' he said sternly. 'Because you no longer worship him, no rain will fall in your country for two years – or maybe even three!'

King Ahab glared down at Elijah from his throne and raised one eyebrow.

'So?' he sneered.

'So,' Elijah continued, 'there will be a severe drought in Israel. You know that if it doesn't rain the crops won't grow, and if there isn't any food there will be a famine.'

'I don't believe you,' laughed the king. 'Anyway, I don't care about your God and you don't scare me!'

'I'm not trying to scare you,' said Elijah patiently. 'I'm simply telling you what's going to happen.'

'Well, I'm not bothered!' the king repeated. 'Get out of here – you're wasting my time!'

'Doesn't it worry you that your people could starve because of what you are doing?' Elijah asked.

'No it doesn't!' roared the king. 'Because I don't believe a word you are saying! If a drought comes to my lands, I've got plenty of other gods to pray to. They will send rain whenever I say so!'

'We'll see!' responded Elijah, gathering up his cloak. 'But remember my warning . . .'

With these words Elijah stalked out of the palace, the

sound of the king's laughter ringing in his ears. He was angry, and upset, because he knew that many innocent people would now suffer as a result of the king's foolishness.

God led him to a special place in the desert – a tiny cave beside a small stream. Here he could sleep at night or shelter from the hot rays of the sun during the day. It was a quiet and peaceful spot, but very lonely! Elijah didn't see anyone for weeks and weeks. The only other living creatures were some ravens. God sent them to his cave, morning and evening, with meat and bread for him to eat.

Day after day the sun beat down from a cloudless blue sky. Just as God had said, there was no rain and the ground became drier and drier, harder and harder. The little stream began to dry up, and soon everywhere was dry and cracked. Elijah now had nothing to drink.

'What am I going to do?' he asked God. 'If I stay here any longer I'll die of thirst.'

'You must go to the town of Zarephath,' God answered. 'I have chosen someone there to look after you.'

So early the next morning Elijah set off. As he trudged along the stony road he noticed how bare the countryside was. The grass and crops were brown and dying – there was nothing to eat! A few thin and scraggy animals were gathered around the few pools of water that remained. By now the sun was a round fiery ball, high in the clear blue sky. As Elijah paused to wipe the perspiration from his face, he knew that the drought would become much, much worse!

Nearing Zarephath he met a woman gathering firewood. She had gathered together a few twigs and branches from the dying trees.

'Could you get me a drink of water?' he asked. 'I have travelled a long way and I'm very thirsty.'

The woman straightened up and turned to face him. She had been startled by the sudden voice, but when she saw the stranger's kind face she realised she had nothing to fear.

'You must be tired too!' she replied. 'Sit here and rest while I get you a drink.'

Elijah glanced about him and headed for the shade of a nearby tree, welcoming the chance to rest his tired feet.

Meanwhile the woman bundled up her firewood and turned towards her home. But she'd only taken a few steps when Elijah called after her.

'And bring me some bread too – I'm terribly hungry! I haven't eaten for days!'

The woman stopped and then returned to him with her load, dropping the sticks at his feet.

'I can give you a drink, sir, but I can't give you any bread – I haven't any!'

'But I'm hungry!' protested Elijah.

'Yes – well, so am I,' she replied. Who did this fellow think he was! Creeping up behind people and asking for food from a perfect stranger?

'Don't you know there is a drought?' she asked aloud, waving her arms about.   'Look around you – do you see any crops growing? No! There is nothing to eat and there hasn't been anything for ages! All I have left in my kitchen is a handful of flour and a few drops of olive oil in a jar.'

'Surely that's enough to make bread for your husband and the two of us?' ventured Elijah.

'My husband is dead,' said the woman shortly. 'And I have a small son to provide for. We are very poor, and this will be our last meal. I was collecting firewood so I could cook it. After today we'll have nothing – we will starve!'

'Go and prepare your meal,' said Elijah, standing up and placing his hand on her shoulder. 'But first make me a little loaf of bread, and then use the rest of the flour and oil to make bread for yourself and your son.'

The widow angrily pushed his hand away, staring at him in disbelief.

'Haven't you been listening to me?' she exclaimed. 'If you want food you've come to the wrong person! I told you – there is not enough for my son and I! How do you expect me to share it amongst three?'

'You will have enough, I promise,' the prophet responded calmly.

'You promise!' she cried. 'How can that be possible? Be

practical, man! I am poor – if there was more food to be had, which there isn't, I wouldn't have the money to buy it! Once it's gone it's gone – I have no more.'

'Don't worry,' Elijah consoled her. 'God has sent me here to stay with you, and I promise that while I remain here, your bowl won't run out of flour nor your jar out of olive oil.'

'Haven't you been listening to a word I have said?' she retorted angrily. 'If you stay here you will starve – with my son and I.'

'We'll see! You will be surprised . . . '

She glared at him for a minute before bending down to pick up her firewood again.

'You had better come with me – if this is our last meal it won't really matter whether it is divided into two or three! Come and share what we have. I am Rachel and you are welcome in my home.'

As they reached the house a young boy met them at the door.

'Hello, Mum. Did you find . . .' He stopped when he saw the strange man standing behind his mother, wondering who he was.

Elijah had been living in the desert for a long time. He was dusty, his clothes were ragged, and his tangled hair and beard badly needed washing and combing! The boy glanced at his mother as the stranger smiled and followed her into the house. Whatever was she doing, bringing this peculiar man into their home?

'This is my son, Reuben,' the widow told Elijah. She turned to the boy, who was eyeing Elijah curiously. 'This man has come to eat with us,' she explained. 'His name is Elijah, so you talk with him while I prepare our meal.'

She hauled her bundle of sticks into the kitchen to light the fire while Reuben led Elijah to the other room where they sat down. Reuben said nothing but simply stared at the visitor, who, tired after his long walk, simply closed his eyes and dozed. When he saw that Elijah was asleep, Reuben wandered into the kitchen where his mother was making bread from the last of their flour and oil.

'Who is that man?' he asked her, sniffing the baking bread hungrily.

'Where did he come from?'

'Shhh! You'll wake him up!' His mother glanced in the direction of the other room anxiously. 'He says he comes from God,' she whispered. 'He has come to share our food with us.'

'Why come to us?' Reuben exclaimed. 'We don't have much! Surely he'd have been better off going to someone who is rich?'

She shrugged her shoulders as she carefully lifted the golden bread out of the oven. It smelled delicious!

'We must share what we have, as little as it is,' she told him firmly.

Reuben watched as she placed the small loaf of bread on the table to cool. He sighed deeply as he wandered out of the kitchen, knowing that now instead of half a loaf he was only going to have a third! He loved his mother very much, but why did she have to be so generous – especially when they had so little?

The small group didn't say much as they sat down to their meal. Reuben ate his food quickly because he was so hungry, but his mother ate slowly, trying to make her final meal last as long as possible. Elijah didn't appear worried at all and seemed to really enjoy his bread!

Rachel cleared the table after their meal was finished. As she placed the plates in the kitchen she glanced at the empty bowl and jar on the table, wondering if they'd ever be used again. Then she gasped and peered even closer.

The poor widow could hardly believe what she was seeing! There, before her very eyes, was a bowl of flour and a jug of olive oil – exactly the same as before she had prepared the meal! She shook her head slightly, wondering if she was dreaming, and rubbed her eyes with her hand. The flour and the olive oil remained exactly where they were!

'Reuben . . . Reuben! Come here quickly!' she called to her son, her voice shaking with excitement. He came rushing into the room.

Rachel's finger trembled as she pointed to the bowl and jar on the table.

'I used all the flour and oil to make that bread,' she spluttered. 'But now the bowl and the jug are both full up again – look!'

Reuben glanced at his mother and then peered into the two containers. Sure enough there was flour and oil in both of them!

'Perhaps you didn't quite use it all . . .' he suggested, frowning.

'I did – I know I did! I used every bit – but now there's still the same amount left! I don't understand . . .'

A slight rustling made her turn around, and there in the doorway she saw Elijah, smiling down at her.

'I told you God would look after us . . . Your bowl won't run out of flour and your jar won't run out of oil until it rains again! God has promised this because of your kindness to me.'

Rachel stared at him open-mouthed. She still could hardly believe the evidence there in front of her – but of one thing she was certain. They still had enough flour and oil for tomorrow! Could his promise be true after all?

'You must stay with us until this drought is over,' she said firmly.

Reuben glanced from one to the other, then at the bowl and jar. He shook his head. He still thought Rachel must have made a silly mistake . . .

As the days passed though, he began to change his mind. He watched closely as his mother made their daily meal from the flour and oil. He saw her mix it all together and then cook the loaf – yet there was always some flour and oil left for the next day's meal! Soon he realised, as his mother had done earlier, that their visitor was a very special person!

'He is a man of God,' his mother whispered one day in answer to his question. 'He will make sure we have enough to eat during this terrible drought.'

Day after day the sun kept shining, baking the ground hard and drying up the last few streams. Although there was still no sign of rain, Rachel, Reuben and Elijah had food to eat, for the flour and oil never failed to appear in the bowl and jar every day. Their meals weren't feasts – but they were enough to keep them going . . .

One day, however, Reuben came into the house holding his stomach.

'I don't feel very well . . .' he told his mother faintly.

Rachel placed her hand on his hot forehead and peered into his pale face.

'You had better lie down for a while,' she said. 'Perhaps your temperature will go down after you've had a sleep and something to drink.'

She took him to his room and Reuben lay down on his bed. His mother nursed him all day and night – but he grew worse and worse! Nothing she did seemed to have any effect . . .

Then one day Elijah found Rachel alone in the kitchen.

'What's wrong, Rachel?' he asked, placing his hand lightly on her shoulder. 'Isn't Reuben any better?'

She stood up, pushing his hand away. Elijah could now see her eyes, and although they were filled with tears they were also filled with anger.

'Any better?' she cried out in anguish. 'My son is dead – dead! It's all your fault!'

Elijah stared at her in horror. He had never thought that this would happen.

'We were all right by ourselves until you came along! I did my best to help you and now look what's happened! What thanks is this? It's true we have had enough to eat just as you promised, but what good is that now? It would have been better if we'd starved weeks ago. What is to become of me now? I have no husband and no son to look after me – I am all alone, and it's all your fault!'

She collapsed back into her chair, weeping bitterly. Her face was hidden in her hands and her whole body shook with grief. She had been through so much, and now this! Why hadn't this stranger just left them alone?

Elijah replaced a comforting hand on her shoulder. 'Where is the boy?' he whispered, tears choking his voice.

Rachel didn't answer and he wasn't sure if she'd heard him or not. She continued crying, so he left her and went to Reuben's bedroom. Tears filled his eyes as he saw the small body lying so still on the bed. Elijah picked him up and carried him to his own room, where he lay him down. He then knelt on the floor and prayed in a loud, sad voice.

'Oh God, why has this happened? This poor woman has helped me and cared for me, and now you have taken away her only child. She has done so much for me! Oh God, please bring this boy back to life!'

Elijah then lay on top of Reuben, stretching himself over the lifeless body. Three times he called out to God, begging him to bring the child back to life. After the third time Elijah stood beside the bed, waiting and watching closely. His old face broke into a smile of relief as he saw Reuben stir.

'Thank God – he's breathing!' he exulted. 'He is alive! Oh thankyou – thankyou God!'

Reuben sat up, rubbing his eyes. 'What am I doing in your room?' he demanded, realising where he was.

Elijah just grinned at him. 'How do you feel?' he asked.

'I'm all right,' Reuben replied. 'In fact I don't feel sick any more . . .'

'Let's go and find your mother,' smiled Elijah as he hugged the bewildered boy. He grabbed him by the hand, and together they ran to the kitchen where Rachel was still sitting sobbing. Her head was buried in her hands just as when Elijah had left her.

'Look Rachel, your son is alive!'

Her body froze and she looked up angrily.

'How dare you make such a cruel . . .' Her outburst ceased when she saw Reuben standing, alive and well, behind Elijah!

'Oh – oh!' she cried, rushing to her son, her arms outstretched to hug and kiss him. 'Thank God – it's a miracle . . . a miracle!'

'What's all the fuss about?' asked Reuben, struggling free of her caresses. Had his mother finally taken leave of her senses!

'What does he mean about me being alive? I know I was sick . . .'

But no one answered him. His mother continued to hold him tightly and would not to let him go. At last she raised her eyes from Reuben's face and gazed at Elijah.

'Oh sir,' she said. 'Now I really know you are a man of God! I'm so sorry for the things I said to you! I was upset – I didn't mean them! Thank you for giving me my son back . . .'

'It was God who returned him to you, Rachel,' the prophet replied. 'Not me!'

Rachel held out a hand to Elijah. 'You are welcome to stay here as long as you wish,' she told him warmly.

'Thank you, Rachel,' he smiled. 'I will like that . . .'

The three of them stood together, with Reuben staring from his mother to Elijah. He was still puzzled. Something wonderful had happened that they both knew about, but he didn't understand. Perhaps, one day, they'd tell him all about it!

The woman who had everything

Elisha was a prophet – a messenger from God – who travelled around Israel. It was hot and Elisha had been travelling all day but now his destination was near. The countryside was dry and the road dusty. He decided that he would go straight to the well in Shunem – a small town in the north of the country.

As he walked along the road he noticed a woman coming towards him. He was about to pass her when she spoke to him.

'Err – Excuse me, sir,' she asked hesitantly. 'I hoped I would meet you today. Are you hungry?'

Her question greatly surprised him. What a strange way to greet a complete stranger in the middle of the street! She spoke as if she knew him – but he was certain he had never met her before in his life. And what a question! Was he hungry? He couldn't remember the last time he'd eaten a proper meal.

'I would like you to come and share a meal with us,' the woman continued, not waiting for him to reply. 'We have more than enough food for ourselves, and my husband would be delighted to have you as our guest.'

Elisha didn't know what to say. The woman's dress told him that she was very rich – her softly flowing robes were made from the most costly material, and there were expensive looking jewels on her fingers and around her neck. Elisha glanced down at his own rough clothes. Why had she invited him to come and eat at her home?

'I'm sorry,' he stammered, 'but I don't know who you are. I think you have mistaken me for someone else.'

The woman smiled and shook her head.

'There's no mistake. I've seen you in Shunem many times, and heard that you're a man of God, but I've never had the chance to speak to you. I suppose my question was a bit sudden – but I wasn't sure how to begin! My name is Leah, and my husband is Jethro. We would be pleased if you'd come and eat with us today – if you would like to, of course.'

Would he like it! Elisha smiled to himself. During his wanderings throughout the land he was never sure when, or where, he would eat his next meal. He very rarely had the chance to sit down at a table and enjoy really good food!

'Well, thank you!' he exclaimed. 'That would make a lovely change!'

Elisha set off with the woman to her home, a large white building on the edge of the town. There were tall sycamore trees around the house which provided plenty of shade from the fierce sun.

'I have invited this man to eat with us,' she explained to her husband as they entered the house. 'His name is Elisha.'

Jethro nodded a welcome. If he was surprised by Elisha's odd clothing he was too polite to show it. 'We are pleased to have you here,' was all he said.

Leah clapped her hands and several servants, dressed in white, hurried into the room.

'Show our guest where he can wash before we begin eating,' she commanded them sharply. She turned to Elisha. 'If there is anything you want, you have only to ask . . .'

The servants led Elisha up the elegant stairway. They glanced back at him curiously, and then looked at each other. They didn't dare say anything – but they did wonder where their mistress had found such a strange looking man!

Elisha stared straight in front of him, feeling rather awkward. He certainly didn't look as if he belonged in these opulent surroundings! His harsh robe was ragged and dirty, his feet were dusty, and one of his sandals was held together with a piece of string! His long hair and beard were tangled, untidy and matted.

When he reappeared a little later to be greeted by Leah and Jethro, his robe and sandals were still the same, but his face, hands and feet were now washed and clean. His hair and beard had been combed neatly and were still damp.

'That feels much better,' he informed them gratefully. 'I feel almost human again!'

Elisha felt even better after he had eaten his meal! He didn't seem to want to leave, but at last he rose and thanked his hosts for their kindness.

'We'd be pleased if you came to eat with us every time you're in Shunem,' said Leah.

'Or even if you're just passing by,' Jethro added.

Elisha put on his ragged cloak. 'That's very kind of you,' he told them. 'I'll look forward to that very much indeed.'

Leah led him to the door. As he walked briskly down the road leading out of town, he turned once and waved goodbye. Leah waved back.

'I'm sure he is a holy man,' she said to her husband as she rejoined him at the table. 'There is something very special about him . . .'

Jethro nodded. 'I don't think it can be a very comfortable life, wandering around the countryside day after day, never knowing where your next meal will come from.'

They fell silent, comparing Elisha's hard life with the comfort and riches they knew and enjoyed.

'I have an idea . . .' Leah suddenly announced. She hesitated.

'Go on,' Jethro smiled. 'Tell me!'

'Well – why don't we build a room on the top of our house just for him?' Leah asked excitedly. 'We could even put some furniture and a lamp in it! Oh, it doesn't need to be very fancy – but it would be somewhere he could stay whenever he was in Shunem – a place to call his own! He could come and go as he liked, whenever he wanted . . .'

Jethro thought for a moment. 'I think that sounds like a good idea,' he said slowly. His face brightened.

'We can arrange for some clean clothes for him as well – he could certainly do with them!'

They both grinned at each other as they remembered Elisha's dress.

'I'll go out this afternoon and talk to some workmen,' Jethro decided. 'We'll start work on it as soon as possible.'

Leah laughed happily. 'Won't he be in for a surprise?'

Elisha certainly was surprised the next time he came to Shunem! When the excited couple showed him his newly finished room and invited him to stay there he could hardly believe how kind they had been! Shyly he went up the stairs to look at his new surroundings – he could see that the couple had spent a lot of money making it bright and welcoming. He was grateful that now he would have the chance to wash and to sleep in a bed – and to dress in clean clothes now and again! What a wonderful surprise!

The servants soon became used to this stranger coming in at odd times and disappearing just as suddenly. They became used to his odd clothes as well! Sometimes Elisha came to the house alone and at other times he brought his own servant Gehazi with him.

During one of his visits, Elisha asked Gehazi to bring the mistress of the house up to him.

'Is anything wrong, Elisha?' Leah asked worriedly, as she entered the room. 'I hope none of my servants has been rude to you, or perhaps the food . . .'

He held up his hand for her to stop, a wide grin on his face.

'No, no,' he said. 'Nothing is wrong. The servants do anything for me, the food is excellent – and this room is wonderful! That's why I want to talk to you . . .'

Although she was relieved that there was nothing wrong, Leah was puzzled. 'How can I help you then?'

Elisha chuckled. 'That's the question I wanted to ask you! You have been so kind and done so much for me that I would like to repay you in some way. I haven't any money – but is there some other way in which I can say thank you?'

Leah smiled at her new friend and shook her head.

'You know I am a rich woman,' she told him. 'I have many servants who make life easy for me, and my house is very comfortable. My husband and I are happy – and we both enjoy having you here! Thank you, Elisha, but I really don't think there's anything I could possibly need . . .'

Elisha nodded his head slowly as she left the room. He turned to his servant, who stood nearby.

'What do you think, Gehazi? Is it true that she doesn't want anything at all?'

Gehazi put his head on one side as he thought for a moment.

'It's true that she can buy anything she wants,' he replied, 'but there are some things money can't buy . . . I know that she and her husband don't have any children, and she would dearly love a son. Does that help?'

Elisha nodded. 'I knew there must be something. Ask her to come back to me, please.'

Leah returned to Elisha's room, puzzled, and a little annoyed at all the coming and going! Perhaps Elisha wasn't feeling very well, she thought. He had never behaved this way before – he usually just kept himself to himself.

Elisha came straight to the point. 'My servant tells me there is something you would like to have.'

She waited, her raised eyebrows asking a silent question.

'I understand you want a son more than anything else,' he continued.

Leah looked first at Elisha and then at Gehazi. How did they find that out? No one except Jethro knew of her secret wish – and he wouldn't have told anyone. The servants must have overheard them talking and whispered amongst themselves.

'I can tell you now that your wish will be granted,' Elisha went on. 'I promise that by this time next year you will be holding a baby boy in your arms.'

Leah burst into peals of laughter as she stared at the two men before her. Then her face grew serious.

'You shouldn't joke or lie like that,' she told Elisha. 'You are a man of God. And anyway, what you say is impossible.'

'You will see that nothing is impossible for God!' called Elisha as Leah made her way out of the room.

As she walked slowly down the stairs, Leah thought hard about what Elisha had said. Even though she had laughed she felt deeply hurt. This man had lied to her about something important – something that was very private. She thought a man of God would have more feelings than that! It was true – she did so much want a son, but she knew it was impossible – quite impossible!

A year later however, the impossible happened – Elisha's promise came true!

As she lay cradling her tiny son in her arms, Leah turned to her husband who sat smiling beside her.

'I feel so ashamed,' she murmured, stroking the baby's soft, downy head. 'I laughed when Elisha told me I'd have a child – and here I am with a son! I should have believed him – I know that now. This is the most wonderful thing that has happened to me! Oh, Jethro, I'm so happy . . .

Jethro smiled proudly at his little son.

'I'm happy too,' he said, 'and I think David is just the right name for him.' Gently he touched the baby's chin with his finger. 'We're going to have lots of fun together, little man.'

For several years the little family lived very happily. When David grew old enough, he would often go with his father into the fields to watch the men working and play among the tall stalks of corn.

One morning as the workers were harvesting the crop, David, who had been playing quietly by himself, suddenly cried out, holding his head in his hands.

'Father! Father – my head hurts! Oh, it hurts so much!'

Jethro looked round from where he had been speaking with his foreman to see his son rolling about on the ground.

'What's wrong, son?' he cried as he ran towards him. 'What's the matter?'

'My head! My head hurts!' David repeated, groaning and crying at the same time.

'Quickly!' Jethro ordered two servants. 'Carry him back to the house and give him to his mother. Hurry – but be careful!'

Leah heard David's cries even before he was brought into the house. She rushed to meet him, her face white and anxious.

'What's wrong with him?' she gasped, clutching the arm of the servant. 'Oh quickly, tell me what's happened!'

'We don't know, Mistress,' panted the servant, who had hurried all the way back from the corn fields. 'One minute he was playing happily near us, and the next he was rolling on the ground, screaming!'

'The Master told us to bring him back to you,' added the other servant. 'He said he will be here as soon as he can.'

Leah felt her son's forehead and ordered them to take him to his room. She led the way, and then settled herself into a chair. 'Give him to me,' she said as she stretched out her arms.

Gently they lowered the limp figure onto her lap. Leah cuddled her little boy close, rocking him backwards and forwards and crooning gently in his ear. She nodded for the servants to leave.

The child's sobbing quietened as his mother brushed his damp hair from his forehead with her hand. She whispered soothingly to him all the time as she rocked him back and forth, back and forth. Eventually, his sobs ceased altogether, and he seemed to pass into a deep, trance-like sleep.

Leah smiled down at the still little form, thankful that his crying had ended, that his pain seemed to have been eased. The smile froze on her face as the awful truth dawned on her: her precious little son was not sleeping – he was dead!

She couldn't believe it – was it only a few hours ago that she had sent him out into the fields to burn off all that excess energy . . . How could it be? She didn't know what to do.

The death of the son she had wanted for so long left her numb. She knew that he had died but . . .

Without realising what she was doing, Leah carried the little body up to Elisha's room and laid him on the bed. As she bent over and kissed his damp forehead, Leah heard the anxious voice of her husband calling.

'Leah! Leah! Where are you? How is he?' But as she came down the stairs he knew that the news wasn't good.

'He's dead,' she said sadly, as she brushed back a few loose hairs from her cheek. 'There was nothing I could do.'

They didn't feel like talking and didn't know what to do. They just sat down and stared at the floor. All they could think about was the happy little boy of yesterday, who had been full of life – but who was now lying still, no longer breathing. Although they were heartbroken, they were too shocked to cry – the tears wouldn't flow.

Suddenly Leah stood up and faced Jethro, a strange expression on her face.

'I want one of the servants to bring me a donkey,' she announced.

'What do you want a donkey for?' he asked amazed. 'This is no time to go for a ride!' What could she be thinking of?

'I'm going to find Elisha, he'll know what to do! I'll be back as soon as I can.'

'Why do you have to go now, after what has happened? Whatever are you thinking of? What good will he be to us?'

'Never mind,' she said, 'but I'm going now.'

'You'll never find him! You don't even know where he is,' Jethro added.

'He said he was going to Mount Carmel, so I'll try there.'

Her decision made, she called for the servants to prepare a donkey and she was soon on her way.

She was still some distance from the mountain when Elisha, who had seen the donkey approaching, recognised her.

'Gehazi, look! It's Leah, the Shunammite!'

'Yes sir, I think you are right!

'I want you to hurry down to meet her,' said Elisha, 'and find out if everything is all right with her and her family.'

Elisha was worried as he watched Gehazi scramble down the hill to meet the donkey and its rider. There must be some reason for Leah to come out here, in the desert, to find him, he thought.

'Is there anything wrong at home?' Gehazi asked the dusty traveller when he had caught his breath.

'No,' she replied. 'There's nothing wrong at all . . . but I would like to see Elisha.'

If Gehazi had looked closely he would have seen how upset she was. But he just shrugged his shoulders and led her to Elisha. Reaching him she jumped from her donkey and fell at his feet, catching hold of them. Surprised and shocked at this, Gehazi stepped forward quickly to push her away, but Elisha held him back firmly.

'Leave her alone,' he said. 'Can't you see she's distraught. The Lord hasn't spoken to me, I must know what's wrong.'

Gehazi stepped back and watched in silence. The tears were now cascading down Leah's cheeks, cleaning away the dust that had stuck to her face.

'I didn't ask you to give me a son,' she burst out. 'I told you I was happy enough. But you had to be kind and change my life! Well now he's dead and . . . and it's all your fault!'

Turning to Gehazi, Elisha held out his staff. 'Take this and go straight to the house. Run as fast as you can and don't stop to talk to anyone on the way. Do you understand?'

Gehazi nodded and took the staff.

'When you get to the house, find the boy and hold my stick over him.'

Nodding again, Gehazi ran towards Shunem, clutching the gnarled staff tightly in his hand. Elisha and Leah followed him as fast as they could.

Gehazi was out of breath when he arrived at the house. Not stopping to rest he ran up the stairs and held the staff over the still body, but nothing happened. David lay as still and lifeless as when Leah had left the room.

Hearing Elisha and Leah arrive, he ran downstairs to meet them.

'I did as you requested,' he told his master. 'I held your staff over the boy, but nothing happened. He didn't wake up.'

Still puffing, Elisha glanced at Leah beside him and placed a comforting hand on her arm.

'I'll go up by myself,' he said softly. 'Wait here and don't be afraid.'

Taking the stairs two at a time, Elisha rushed to his room. Tears came to his eyes when he saw David's body lying deathly still on the bed. Gently he closed the door and crossed the room.

Although he had been praying on the journey back from Mount Carmel, Elisha now asked God again for David to be brought back to life. Then he lay on top of him, placing his mouth, eyes and hands over David's mouth, eyes and hands, and breathed hard. After a couple of minutes he began to feel the warmth return to the boy's cold body. Elisha stood up to look at the boy and then returned to the bed. He again stretched himself out over the child. This time David sneezed several times and opened his eyes. He smiled when he saw Elisha.

'Hello Elisha, what are you doing here? Why am I in your room?' he enquired as he realised where he was.

Elisha laughed and put his arm around the little boy's shoulders.

'You weren't feeling well,' he explained, 'but you're better now, so let's go down to your mother.'

Slowly they descended together as David's legs still felt wobbly.

'Here is your son,' Elisha called out, smiling broadly when he saw the surprised mother.

Leah ran and fell again at Elisha's feet, her head touching the ground, her face wet with tears of joy.

'Oh thank you Elisha!' she repeated over and over again. She then stood and hugged David tightly. 'Are you going to stay with us?' she asked the two men.

Elisha shook his head. 'No, not this time. We must return to Mount Carmel but we'll be back in Shunem soon.'

'Then we must go and find Jethro, and tell him the wonderful news,' she said, and left the room with her arm firmly around David's shoulders.

Elisha and Gehazi smiled as they too left the house, to return to Mount Carmel, praising God for the miracle.

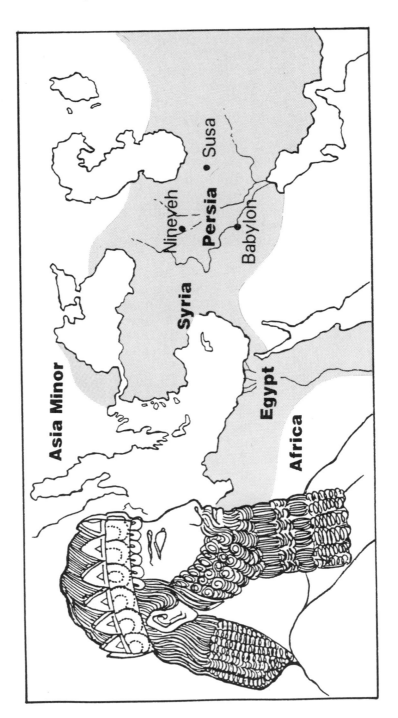

Xerxes' Empire stretched from Libya to India, and from Russia to the Sudan.

Taking a risk

Xerxes, King of Persia, ruled over an enormous empire. His one hundred and twenty seven provinces stretched all the way from India to the islands of Greece, from the shores of the Caspian Sea to the Nubian Desert. He had huge armies under his command, and millions of subjects – Persians, Medes, Lydians and Babylonians . . .

In the third year of his reign Xerxes decided to display his power and riches at a grand exhibition, and the officials of all the provinces of his kingdom were invited to Susa, his splendid capital city. The exhibition lasted for six months, and afterwards there was to be a whole week of feasting in the palace gardens. It was to be the most splendid banquet anyone could remember!

All Xerxes guests marvelled at the luxurious furnishings of his palace. There were colourful hanging screens, fastened with golden cords to the marble columns. The most wonderful furniture glittered as the light from countless lamps reflected on the elaborate polished surfaces. In the courtyards hundreds of fountains played over intricate mosaics of white marble, red feldspar, blue turquoise, shining mother-of-pearl; a whole sea of dazzling colour that seemed to shimmer and move in the sun.

The tables groaned under the weight of food from the farthest corners of the earth. Everything that could be eaten was prepared – the servants staggered under the weight of the dishes they had to carry. Roast ox, lark's tongues in aspic, honeyed dormice, stuffed giraffe necks, boiled sheeps' eyes . . . there was no end to the courses. There were mountains of figs, piles of pomegranates, heaps of candied fruits and enough dates to fill a thousand calenders! There was so much to eat that a month wouldn't have been long enough to sample everything. Wine flowed from morning till night, sipped from golden goblets, no two the same. Everyone was to drink as much as they desired . . .

Meanwhile, inside the harem – the part of the palace set aside for the women – Queen Vashti held a smaller banquet of her own. The wives of all Xerxes' rich and important friends and officials were at her table. Both parties were a huge success and everyone was enjoying themselves immensely

The king never failed to grasp an opportunity to show off his possessions. Towards the end of the week of feasting, he decided it was time to display his greatest prize, Vashti – his queen.

'Tell Bigtha and the other attendants to go to the harem and bring my wife to me,' he commanded. 'She is to come here, dressed in her finery and all her royal regalia – I want to show all the men here what a beautiful woman she is.'

The attendants hurried to the harem where they presented themselves to the queen, who was busy entertaining her guests. Harbona told her of the king's wishes.

'Does he expect me to parade in front of his friends like another of his possessions?' she asked. 'I am the queen, not something to be displayed before them like a prize camel at a bazaar! Tell him I will not come!'

Bigtha and Harbona glanced at one another, unsure what to do next. No one had ever disobeyed the king before and lived to tell the tale! Perhaps, if they waited, she would change her mind . . .

Vashti turned back to her guests and continued her conversation, ignoring the attendants entirely.

'What are you waiting for?' she demanded a little later, noticing that they hadn't departed. 'Didn't you hear what I said? Go on, get out – you're spoiling our meal!'

The attendants backed out, bowing deeply, too frightened to speak – even to each other. They scurried back to the king.

'Well?' Xerxes began, slurring his words slightly as he sipped some more wine. 'When will she arrive? I want her entrance to be as spectacular as possible . . .'

Bigtha stepped forward. 'The . . . the queen says she won't appear.' he stuttered, trembling with fear.

'She says she won't be paraded like a prize animal,' Zethar offered, slightly bolder than his companion.

'What! . . . She said what?' Xerxes stormed. 'How dare she disobey me!' Zethar had to duck quickly to avoid the goblet that the king threw at him in rage – the wine went everywhere, staining Xerxes' fine clothes as well as soaking his servant.

The room was now completely silent. All eyes turned towards the king, whose face had taken on a dangerous purple hue.

Zethar's reply had been heard by everyone present. No one dared speak, but they were all thinking the same thing – what was Xerxes going to do? No one had ever dared disobey the mighty King of the Medes and Persians!

Xerxes thought rapidly. He knew his answer was awaited, and he felt very embarrassed. All these riches and possessions meant nothing in the eyes of these men if his own wife dared to defy him!

'Bring my seven noble advisers to me, at once!' he commanded clearly, so that everyone would hear. 'I, Xerxes the king, have given Queen Vashti an order and she has refused to obey me. What does the law say I should do with her?'

The advisers huddled together to discuss the problem. Immediately a buzz of conversation broke out around the room. The feasting and drinking was forgotten.

These servants carrying food to a banquet were carved beside the steps of Xerxes' palace at Persepolis.

After some discussion the advisers stood before their king. 'Well?' asked Xerxes.

'This is indeed very serious, Oh Xerxes the Magnificent!' Memucan, the spokesman for the seven, began. 'Queen Vashti isn't just insulting you as king – she insults every man present here today!'

There was a murmur of agreement throughout the courtyard.

'If news of the queen's insult becomes known, there will be great problems throughout the whole empire,' Memucan continued. 'Women everywhere will take it as a sign of how they can behave.'

There was much nodding of heads as the men agreed.

'What he says is true,' Shethar and Admatha chorused in agreement.

'My wife is attending the queen's banquet,' Carshena added. 'If Queen Vashti gets away with this, my authority at home will be finished!'

' ''If the queen can refuse her husband, so can I'' – that's what mine will say!' Tarshish finished. 'The queen must be punished, and swiftly, before our wives copy her ideas . . .'

A rowdy chorus greeted these opinions. The guests were eager to hear what was being decided – it would also affect them!

'We suggest, Your Majesty, that you issue a law saying Queen Vashti may never again appear before you,' Memucan proposed. 'Her royal position should be given to someone who is better suited. When your proclamation is made known throughout the empire, every woman will treat her husband with proper respect, whether he's rich or poor.'

Cheers and applause greeted his words. Everyone was relieved that an example was to be made. The law in Persia and Media was official and could not be changed, so Queen Vashti and all other wives would be put in their places, once and for all!

'I will accept your advice,' said the king, and the advisers went off to write out the new law. The guests relaxed and feasted with even greater enthusiasm.

Later, when the king's anger had subsided, Marsena, another adviser, approached. 'May I make a suggestion, your majesty?' he asked.

'Certainly,' Xerxes replied with little interest. Slowly he ran a ringed finger around the rim of his gold cup.

'When Vashti has gone, you'll need a new queen,' Marsena began. There was no reply so he continued. 'Why don't you organise a beauty contest for all the girls in the empire? The loveliest can then be brought to the harem, and you can choose your queen from amongst them.'

Xerxes sat silently for a moment and then looked up, grinning.

'That's an excellent idea,' he enthused. 'I'll get my servant, Hegai, to organise it immediately!'

Feeling a great deal more cheerful, Xerxes rejoined the banquet, laughing and joking with his guests as if nothing had happened.

The celebrations were finally over. The officials and their wives left to return to their homes, scattered throughout the empire. No one noticed another figure leave the palace – the slight figure of Vashti, mounted on a donkey, returning home to her parents. She had lost her crown and title of queen but she had not lost her dignity. She held her head high, knowing she had proved to herself, and others, that she was a person and not just one of the king's possessions.

The beauty contest was proclaimed far and wide. Every young woman in the empire had to enter, and the finalists were brought to Xerxes' harem. Once in the palace the girls spent a whole year on beauty treatments! They were massaged with oils of myrrh and balsam, they learnt how to dress attractively and how to apply exotic perfumes and cosmetics. Finally, Xerxes would summon them one by one into his presence . . .

But as the days and months passed, the king became more and more disgruntled. Even though his harem was now filled with the most exquisite women in the empire, not one of them did Xerxes consider fit to be his queen!

Then one day a new young girl was brought before him – and Xerxes found her much more attractive than any of the others! Not only was she one of the most lovely women he had ever set eyes on, but she was also much brighter than any of the beauties Xerxes had met so far. Sweet smelling oils and exotic costumes were all very well, but sometimes the king began to long for some intelligent conversation . . .

Before long he had installed her in her own private quarters, and shortly afterwards he crowned her as his queen. The name of this special girl was Esther.

Esther had been brought up by her cousin, Mordecai, who had adopted her when her parents had died. He had only given her one piece of advice as she left for the palace. 'Don't tell anyone about your family, Esther,' he warned her. 'Xerxes must not discover that you are a Jew . . .'

Esther had been puzzled by this advice but decided to do as she was instructed. Mordecai had always given her good advice in the past. She also knew that the Jews weren't popular with everyone in the empire. If nothing was said there could be no trouble.

'I'll do as you say, cousin,' she promised, squeezing his hand. 'No one in the palace will ever know . . .'

So Esther was crowned queen. A great banquet was ordered and the whole empire celebrated the marriage of the king and his new queen. A great holiday was declared, and all the citizens of Susa flocked to the palace to congratulate the royal couple.

Now Xerxes was a powerful king, but he was not popular with all of his subjects. Some of them just couldn't wait to get rid of him, and soon after the wedding two of the Royal Guards hatched a plot to assassinate their ruler.

Mordecai, who often sat by the palace gate hoping to hear some news of Esther, was waiting one day when he overheard some of the guards whispering. They were so intent on their conversation that they took no notice of the old man, sitting in the sun with his eyes closed, nearby.

'Bigthana and Teresh are ready,' whispered one guard. 'The king will be taken completely by surprise as he returns from the court . . .'

'It will be over before anyone realises what has happened,' sneered another. 'And Persia's mighty king will be dead!'

They laughed and moved off into the palace grounds without a backward glance.

If they had looked back they would have seen that Mordecai's eyes were now wide open, for he had overheard everything! He realised the king must be warned – but how? He didn't know how many guards were involved in the plot. There was only one answer.

'I'll tell Esther,' he muttered. 'She'll have to warn the king of the danger . . .'

It was difficult for Mordecai to arrange a secret meeting with his cousin, for Queen Esther was hidden away in her own luxurious apartments, and always surrounded by her maid servants and attendants. It involved a lot of careful planning and not inconsiderable danger!

'The king's life is in peril!' he warned, when they managed to meet briefly. 'You must inform him of this plan.'

When Xerxes and Esther were alone that evening, she repeated everything that Mordecai had told her. Xerxes' face became pale, and then suffused with anger as he listened to her story, and as soon as she had finished, he clapped his hands and summoned his most trusted advisors. It wasn't long before the two miserable conspirators were dragged before him.

'You die on the gallows tomorrow, treacherous dogs!' the king declared, and ignoring their pleas for mercy he turned to his officials.

'All Persia shall know of their treason – I want a full account of this matter written down in the official empire records.'

'It shall be done, oh king,' the officials assured him. 'Your word is our command . . .'

Long into the night the royal scribes could be seen writing, on scroll after scroll, a report of how Mordecai had saved the king's life.

Several years passed and the time came for Xerxes to choose a new grand vizier. The new grand vizier would be the most powerful man in the kingdom after the king himself! The man appointed was Haman, a proud and spiteful person.

On the day of his appointment Haman stood before the King, dressed in all his finery.

'Is there anything you would like me to do to celebrate your becoming grand vizier?' Xerxes enquired.

Haman thought for a moment and then smiled smugly.

'I think it's important for everyone in Persia to know how important I am,' he replied. 'Perhaps it would be a good idea if everybody – except you of course, your majesty – were to bow down whenever I pass by.'

The King with his Grand Vizier. From a carving at Persepolis.

The king nodded briefly. 'Very well. I'll write out an order to that effect.'

A servant was called and within an hour, Haman's suggestion had become law. Whenever he walked past anyone, at any time, they were to kneel or bow to him.

Haman wasn't popular in Susa and many people complained among themselves about the new law.

'Who does he think he is?' they muttered. 'Why should we have to bow and scrape to him?'

But Haman was the grand zivier and was very powerful. The people knew that if they disobeyed the new law they would be punished, so they kept their grumbling to themselves and whenever Haman walked along the streets of Susa, or through the corridors of the palace, everyone bowed to him . . . everyone, that is, except Mordecai.

Mordecai stood straight and tall as Haman passed, seemingly unaware of the hatred in the grand vizier's eyes. Every time this happened, Haman grew angrier and angrier. It didn't matter that everyone else in the kingdom obeyed the law – Haman wanted to know why this one man refused.

So too did Haman's friends. One day as they sat talking together, a palace worker turned to Mordecai with a question.

'Why do you refuse to bow to Haman, Mordecai? Don't you know you're breaking the law?'

The others were silent, waiting expectantly for his answer.

'I won't bow down to Haman for one simple reason,' Mordecai informed them. 'I am a Jew and I will only bow down to God.'

The palace workers stared first at Mordecai and then at one another. There were many Jews in Persia, but they hadn't realised Mordecai was one. In fact they hadn't thought about it at all – it had never made any difference before. However, they wondered what Haman would say.

That afternoon two of the palace workers met Haman. One of them spoke hesitantly.

'Oh Mighty Haman, you've probably noticed that one particular man in Susa refuses to bow to you, as the law says he must . . .'

'Yes?' Haman's voice was sharp and suspicious.

'Well, we've found out why he won't,' continued the other worker, his nervous fingers rolling and unrolling the tassel of his robe.

Haman was interested now, but merely raised his eyebrows.

'He says he won't bow to you because he is a Jew,' explained the first man, the words falling anxiously from his lips. 'He says he'll only bow down to his God!'

'Hmmm . . . well, thank you for this information,' mused Haman, one eyebrow twitching as he spoke. 'You may go now . . .'

The two workers hurried away, discussing how calmly Haman had taken the news.

But Haman wasn't really feeling calm! He stalked to his private rooms and furiously slammed the door shut. So that was why that miserable, insignificant little man refused to bow to him! He would show him that the grand vizier of Persia had power over everybody – especially over the Jews! Anger surged through him again as he pictured in his mind the number of times Mordecai had deliberately snubbed him, holding his head high, not bothering to bow. Yes – he would make that Mordecai show respect! He would . . . he would! A nasty sneer crossed the grand vizier's face as he formed a cruel plan – a plan of revenge on Mordecai! He would punish him certainly, but he would also punish every other Jew in Persia! He would see that every Jew in the Kingdom – every man, woman and child – was killed! That would prove to everyone how powerful he was. The laws of Persia were made to be obeyed!

He stood up and strode to the royal chambers. The guards, seeing him approach, immediately opened the huge double doors for him and bowed as he swept by them.

'The Grand Vizier, Your Majesty.' The announcement came from an invisible servant.

The king glanced up from a scroll he was reading and lifted his sceptre, motioning for the servants around him to leave. Once they were alone, Haman moved closer to the king.

'Your majesty, I have discovered some alarming facts . . .'

'Tell me,' replied Xerxes, keen to hear what his chief advisor had to say.

'I have discovered that there is a group of people, scattered throughout your kingdom, who don't obey your rules, but who observe their own laws and customs.'

Xerxes was worried. He trusted Haman and believed everything he said. The thought that he might have been lying never entered his head.

'What can we do about these people?' he ventured.

Haman hesitated, pretending to ponder over the answer and then replied, 'I've thought a great deal about this, your majesty and I feel it isn't safe for you, as king, to have them remain in Persia. Who knows – they might be planning to overthrow you right this moment! It has been known to happen before . . .'

Xerxes looked more and more unsettled. The attempt a few years ago on his life was still fresh in his mind.

'It may sound a bit drastic, sire, but perhaps the best solution would be to have them all . . . removed. If we kill them all now they will never be a problem to us or to anyone else.'

The king was silent. Xerxes was a strong and ruthless ruler, but governing an empire of this size meant he relied heavily on his officials. He trusted Haman completely and usually took his advice. For a few moments he wondered if there could be another answer. Killing all those people did seem rather excessive . . .

The king frowned, deep in thought, and said nothing, so Haman continued: 'I can guarantee that if you do put all these people to death, a huge amount of money – more than 340,000 kilograms of silver – will be added to the empire's treasury.'

Xerxes was convinced. Money was always needed for running his huge kingdom and this enormous amount of silver would be very useful.

'You do what you think best,' he told his second in command, rising to his feet heavily. 'I'll give you my ring, with my seal on it. You can stamp all decrees so everyone will know that what is written is an official order from the king.'

Haman accepted the ring, bowing deeply. He smiled silkily to himself as he left the royal chamber to organize the writing of the decree. His plan had worked – it had all been so easy! Soon his orders would be despatched to every part of the empire, carried by the same messengers who had taken the news of the king's marriage to Esther. In a few months time, on a single day, all Jews in Persia would be destroyed, and their wealth placed in the king's treasury. Revenge was going to be so very sweet . . .

'Now Mordecai will be sorry he didn't bow and show me the proper respect,' Haman gloated as he watched the messengers depart. 'And there's nothing anyone can do about it!'

As the news of the king's decree spread through the empire, the Jews were reduced to panic, wondering why this law had been passed so suddenly. What had they done to make the king so angry that he wanted to kill them? They felt desperate and helpless, and as Haman had said, there was nothing they could do.

Poor Mordecai was frantic. Dressed like his fellow Jews in sack cloth to show that he was in mourning he walked around the city, crying out in despair, until eventually he threw himself down before the palace gates.

Several of Esther's servants saw him there and told their mistress what he was doing.

'Go and find why out he's acting so strangely,' Esther ordered, 'and take some decent clothes for him to wear.'

The servants met Mordecai at the gate, but he shook his head when they showed him the clothes.

'I am mourning the death of all my people,' he told them. 'I won't take off this sack cloth until this terrible law has been repealed.'

The servants glanced at one another, puzzled.

'What law are you talking about?' one asked.

'Haven't you heard?' Mordecai asked in astonishment. 'The king has ordered that on a single day in a few months time, all Jews are to be killed. All of my people will die – for no reason at all!'

Suddenly he ceased moaning and peered strangely at the servants. 'Haven't you heard anything of this at all?'

They shook their heads.

'And what about the queen?' he continued. 'Does she know about this new law?'

Again the servants shook their heads. 'We don't think so,' they faltered. 'She certainly hasn't mentioned it . . .'

'Then you must tell her everything!' he cried urgently. 'Tell her she is the only one who can do something about it! She must beg the king to change his mind!'

The servants returned to the palace and told Esther the disturbing news.

'Your cousin wants you to plead with the king,' her hand maiden finished. 'He says the king must repeal this dreadful law!'

Esther paced up and down in her room, reading and re-reading the copy of the proclamation Mordecai had given the servants to pass on to her.

'What does he hope I can achieve?' she pleaded. 'He knows that the law of Persia forbids anyone from entering the king's chamber without first being invited!'

The servants nodded dumbly. What their queen said was true. If anyone entered the royal presence unasked they would be struck down immediately by the guards, unless the king intervened by holding out his golden sceptre. It didn't matter who it was – even Queen Esther had to obey that rule.

'I don't know when the king will send for me next,' continued Esther, half to herself. 'He has been so busy lately! I haven't seen him for more than a month . . .'

She paced up and down, thinking desperately, and then sent her maid servant back to Mordecai to explain the problems she faced. Soon after, the servant returned.

'What did he say?' Esther asked quickly.

'He said to tell you that just because you live in the palace, it doesn't mean you're safe,' the girl reported. 'If all Jews are to die, you can be sure you will too . . .'

Esther sank down sadly on her velvet couch. 'I know,' she whispered, 'but somehow I can't see Xerxes passing such a terrible law. I feel it must have been someone else's idea . . .'

'But who?' the maid servant asked her, frowning.

'I'm not sure,' said Esther slowly. 'But perhaps Haman had something to do with it . . .' She shivered suddenly. 'I never trusted that man!'

'Mordecai said something else,' the maid servant added. 'He told me that this may be the reason you've been made queen. By speaking out you, and only you, can save your people . . .'

Esther sat up straight, her dark eyes shining, a look of determination on her face.

'Perhaps he's right!' she exclaimed. 'Return to Mordecai and tell him to get all the Jews in Susa together, and to pray and fast for three whole days.'

'What are we going to do, your majesty?' the maid asked her.

'We will all do the same,' replied Esther firmly. 'After three days I will go and see the king and if he decides not to see me then I will die. If I don't try and see him I will die anyway – and thousands of innocent people with me! Go and tell Mordecai now.'

Esther's maid bowed and hurried away to pass on the message. Mordecai immediately left his position at the palace gate to put his part of the plan into action . . .

Three days later Esther made her way to the king's chamber. She had dressed with care in her finest royal robes.

As she approached the huge double doors she took a deep breath. Her heart pounded in her chest and she clenched and unclenched her hands. What would the king do when he saw her?

As the doors were thrown open the king glanced up in amazement. Before him stood his queen, looking even lovelier than ever. Xerxes gazed at her, entranced by her beauty. His beloved wife had done something which no one else in all Persia had dared to do! Xerxes held up his golden sceptre as a sign that she was welcome . . .

'Come in my Queen!' he commanded. 'What is it that you desire? Ask, and it shall be yours!'

Relief flooded over Esther as she entered the room. She

breathed more easily, although she knew the king's advisers were watching warily. What could the queen want so much, they wondered, that she was prepared to risk her life by coming into the royal presence unbidden?

Esther quickly went over her plan again as she glided across the polished marble floor. Even though Xerxes had offered her anything she wanted, she knew he wouldn't feel obliged to keep his word. The king had been known to compliment people in this way before – it made him feel generous and powerful.

'If it please your majesty,' she began, bowing deeply. 'I have come to invite you and Grand Vizier Haman to a special banquet I have prepared for tonight.'

'I'll be delighted to come!' Xerxes smiled at her. 'I have been neglecting you lately, my jewel!'

If the king was surprised at the invitation – especially as Haman was included – he took care not to show it. 'Bigtha!' he bellowed to his faithful servant. 'Have a messenger sent to the Grand Vizier immediately, commanding his presence this evening.'

Xerxes' advisers were even more surprised by this strange request, and stared open mouthed as Esther departed. What could the queen be up to?

Evening came, and the king, Haman and Esther sat down at the banquet together. As they were finishing, Xerxes turned to his wife. He wiped his carefully curled and perfumed beard with a silken napkin

'Now that we have eaten, most ravishing one, tell me what it is you desire. I know you didn't come to the royal chamber today just to ask me to a banquet!' He leant across the low table towards Esther, and placed his hand over hers. 'I will give you anything you ask . . .' he whispered huskily, gazing into Esther's downcast eyes. 'Just name it and it will be yours.'

Esther looked up at him modestly. She noticed that Haman was listening carefully, although he was pretending not to.

'If I have pleased you, sire, and if you would grant my

request, I would like you and Haman to be my guests tomorrow at the banquet I will prepare for you. Then I will explain to your majesty my wishes.'

The king agreed, but he was puzzled and annoyed. If the queen wanted to ask him something, why did Haman have to come along too? Why couldn't he dine alone with his wife?

Haman, on the other hand, was thrilled with the invitation. He gloated to himself as he left the queen's quarters. Not only was he now the second most powerful man in the empire – second only to the king himself – but he had also been asked to dine privately with the royal couple. And not only once, but twice! Even he had never imagined he would be as successful as this – not yet, anyway!

Haman hurried out of the palace and headed for the main gates. It was here that his euphoria began to pale a little, for there stood Mordecai, upright and defiant. Haman felt his stomach knot with fury – he had eaten particularly well at the banquet – but he managed to control his anger. It had been a wonderful, perfect day, and he wouldn't let that impertinent little man ruin it!

Haman's wife Zeresh and some of his friends were waiting for him when he arrived at his home, and the grand vizier lost no time in bragging about his recent success. They clustered around him as he removed the expensive satin turban he had bought especially for the occasion.

'To round it all off,' he boasted, unpinning the glittering topaz clasp, 'the king and I were the queen's only guests! That's how close we've become – the royal couple want to hear my opinion on everything! I can't think of a grand vizier who has been this influential before . . .'

Haman's friends murmured admiringly as he continued:

'. . . Of course, you've probably heard that I've been invited back again tomorrow.' He put his arm round his wife and hugged her to him. Her eyes were wide with adoration.

'I always knew I was destined for power and glory, but never imagined I would be this successful so quickly!'

Zeresh clasped her hands together in front of her chest. 'That's wonderful! Oh, you are clever, darling! Just wait until I tell my friends – they'll be so jealous!'

Haman smiled at her indulgently, and then frowned.

'Only one thing has stopped tonight from being perfect. That infernal man Mordecai still fails to pay homage to me! How can I enjoy my position and status when he gets away with this insubordination? It's intolerable!'

Zeresh patted his arm reassuringly.

'I agree, darling,' she comforted him. 'The way he snubs you is insufferable!'

'Something will have to be done about him!' one of Haman's friends interjected. 'I can't wait for the pogrom to begin . . .'

Haman nodded, and his wife butted in:

'I've an idea! Why not arrange to have him executed for insubordination tomorrow morning? With your influence it won't be any problem! Then he won't be able to insult you any more.'

Haman thought about this suggestion. 'I do believe it's possible!' He paced up and down the room, becoming more enthusiastic by the minute.

'Yes, it's a brilliant idea! Why didn't I think of it sooner!' Zeresh smiled modestly, not liking to contradict her husband.

'I'll have a gallows built immediately – in our own garden! I think we ought to do this properly. Now . . . let me see . . . let's make it twenty-two metres high! I want everyone to be able to see how we deal with trouble makers in Persia!'

'That's wonderful!'

'Oh Haman, you're so clever!'

'We should have done this months ago!' chorused his cronies.

'Now you'll be able to go to the banquet happy, knowing that disgraceful man is dead, my sweetest,' Zeresh oozed, pleased that the solution had been so easy.

Now that everything was settled Haman called his servants.

'I want a twenty-two metre gallows built ready for a hanging tomorrow. Understood? It is to be a special occasion and I want everyone to be able to see it!'

The servants bowed deeply before their master.

'Yes sir,' they assured him. 'We'll start work on it right away.

So Haman went to bed, confident that by tomorrow night his enemy would live no more . . .

The king, however, couldn't sleep. He tossed and turned, sighing and kicking off the satin coverlet. In the end he gave up. He put on his bejewelled night-robe, slumped in a velvet covered chair and called his servant.

'Abagtha! Abagtha, where are you?'

'Here I am, oh master! What is it that you desire?'

'I desire some sleep,' the king snarled sarcastically, 'although it doesn't look as if I'm going to get any! Get out of here and go to the record-chamber. Perhaps if you read a particularly boring old tablet to me I'll start to feel sleepy! Go on!' he added, as the servant stared at him in bewilderment. 'I don't care which one it is!'

Abagtha disappeared for a few minutes, and Xerxes continued to slouch in his chair, drumming his fingers on the arm in irritation.

'Well?' he snapped, as the servant re-appeared.

'I found these in the back of a cupboard, Your Majesty,' Abagtha faltered, blowing the dust from an especially dull looking armful. 'They're awfully heavy!'

'I'm not interested in where they came from,' replied the king curtly. 'Just read them!'

Abagtha began to read from the first clay tablet. His voice was certainly dreary enough, but the story, instead of sending Xerxes off to sleep, made him sit up and open his eyes! It was the record of how Mordecai had uncovered Bigthana and Teresh's plot to kill the king, and the king became more attentive by the moment.

'I remember this!' he exclaimed, as the weary reader had finished the last tablet. 'That man saved my life!'

'Yes, Your Majesty,' the servant replied heavily.

'The record doesn't say how this man was honoured or rewarded,' added Xerxes. 'Tell me, what did I do for him?'

'Nothing as far as I know, Your Majesty.'

'Nothing! Then we must change that immediately!' the king decided.

Xerxes gazed out of the open window at his capital city, and thought again that dawn was probably when it was at it's most beautiful. The rosy light gave the stone buildings a warm pinkish tinge, and the whole eastern sky was awash with colour. It was extraordinarily peaceful.

'Are any of my officials in the palace yet?' he asked as Carkas, another servant, entered.

'Yes, Your Majesty. I saw the grand vizier a few minutes ago.'

'Good,' said Xerxes. 'Bring him here to me at once.'

Xerxes threw himself down in his chair again and waited for his grand vizier.

Haman entered the room and bowed deeply. He had

already been on his way to see the king when the servant told him he was wanted.

'Your Majesty . . .' he smiled. 'You wish to see me? And how can your humble servant be of assistance?'

'I need your advice . . .'

Haman glowed. It was wonderful to hear the king ask for his advice! He had hoped to be able to ask for Mordecai's death immediately, but perhaps if he could help the king sort out something complicated, he would look even more favourably on his most important advisor! He might even reward me for removing this traitor, Haman thought.

'There's someone in my kingdom whom I want to honour,' said Xerxes. 'What do you suggest I do for this man? It has to be something that is very special!'

Who could the king possibly want to honour so highly, Haman wondered? The answer had to be himself! Only he was deserving of such honours! But he must be careful – he didn't want the king to realise that he had guessed. Xerxes wouldn't like to have his surprise announcement spoiled.

'Honour a man in your kingdom?' he asked rubbing his chin in deliberation. 'There is only one possible way to do this, your majesty! Dress him in some of your own royal robes, place him on one of your own horses, and order one of your highest nobles to lead him through the streets of Susa, crying out for all to hear: ''This man is being honoured by the king, for he has done such wonderful deeds!'' '

As he waited for the king's reply, Haman grinned smugly. He could picture the scene in his mind – it was delightful! Who would he choose to lead him? Mares, Marsena . . . or perhaps Memucan – he had rather stately bearing. He should have suggested having more than one – and possibly an elephant rather than one of the king's horses – that would have been even better! And everyone would be bowing and scraping! It was going to be marvellous . . .

'That's a wonderful idea!' The king's voice interrupted his daydream. 'You can fetch the robe and horse and carry out all your instructions.'

'Me!' Haman's face paled as he stared at Xerxes. 'Who . . . who is the man you wish to honour?' He could hardly speak! How could there be anyone else who deserved such honours? He'd have to do something to prevent this rival from becoming too powerful . . .

'Why, Mordecai the Jew!' the king said simply. 'You'll find him sitting near the gate of the palace, I believe.'

Haman couldn't believe his ears! He was going to pretend to be surprised at the king's announcement, but now his shock and horror were quite genuine. He stood there speechless, rooted to the spot.

'What's the matter? Why haven't you gone?' Xerxes asked impatiently. 'I have given you a royal command. Obey it!'

Numbly Haman bowed and backed slowly to the door. This morning he should have finished off Mordecai, once and for all! Now his plans were in ruins. He could hardly ask for permission to hang the upstart now! He opened the door and stumbled blindly down the corridor to carry out the king's commands.

'It's a good job I didn't carry out Zeresh's idea immediately,' he muttered. 'Stupid woman! If I had disposed of that Jewish wretch I would really have been for it! And upon my own gallows too! Phew, that was a close escape . . .'

In a daze, Haman collected the robes, saddled the horse, and stalked off to the astounded Mordecai. He couldn't bring himself to explain to him what was going on! Only when he rode before him through the streets of Susa did he raise his voice, and that was to declare: 'See how the king honours and rewards this faithful man!'

Haman's dream had turned into a nightmare! As quickly as he could, he finished his chore and hurried home, shamed and embarrassed. His wife and cronies listened to his tale and shook their heads.

'This Mordecai is going to become very powerful,' one asserted. 'If you aren't careful he'll wangle his way into your position . . .'

The words rang in Haman ears. All the time he was dressing for the evening banquet he kept reliving his humiliating experience. He had planned that by this time Mordecai would be dead, and he would be celebrating his triumph. However, events had turned out rather badly. 'The gods are not looking favourably on me today!' he muttered.

Once again the banquet was wonderful, and when it was over, Xerxes again turned to his queen. 'Lily of the Euphrates – tell me what it is that you desire! Were it even half of my kingdom I could not deny you! Tell me, my pearl, why have you invited me to these banquets and teased me so?'

Esther decided that the right time had come. Taking a deep breath, she spoke. 'If it please Your Majesty to grant my humble request, I wish that my people – and I – may live.

Because of your decree we are under threat of being slaughtered!'

She fell to the ground, clasping her husband's knees. Her long, shining hair had become unfastened and streamed over her shoulders and her dark eyes were brimming with tears.

'I could not bear to think I should never see you again, my lord – my husband. But this law says that every one of us shall be destroyed . . .'

Xerxes stared down at her in surprise, almost speechless.

'Who . . . who dares to say my wife be put to the slaughter?'

Esther slowly turned her eyes from the king and glanced from beneath lowered lashes at the grand vizier.

'Our persecutor and enemy is this evil, self-seeking parasite – Haman'

Haman, who had been listening attentively, stared at her in disbelief.

'I . . . I don't understand,' Xerxes spluttered. 'What . . . what are you talking about?'

'He has passed a law that says all Jews are to be killed on a special day this year,' Esther told him, ignoring Haman entirely. 'Well, that means that he has ordered my death because I, too, am a Jew . . .'

Haman's jaw dropped and he stared at her speechless.

'What!' Xerxes roared, jumping to his feet. He overturned the low table in his fury, scattering golden plates and goblets in every direction. He roared again, inarticulately, and stormed out to the gardens, where he began to take out his anger on the plants. A few minutes later he stood in the doorway panting heavily and looking at the scene of destruction, wondering where he could find somewhere quiet to sit and think . . .

Indoors, Esther remained on her couch, listening to the sound of her husband's fury. Outwardly she appeared confident but inside she was uncertain. How strong a hold did Haman have over the king? What would her husband decide?

The terrified Haman, meanwhile, felt sure of what the King's decision would be. For quite a time he was rooted to the spot, too frightened and shocked to move. Like most bullies, he was also a coward. He didn't dare to speak to Xerxes, but he thought that perhaps he could appeal to Esther. He pulled himself to his feet and stumbled towards her couch, where he threw himself at her feet.

'Oh please, please, my queen . . .' he blubbered. 'I had no idea! To think that a fine, noble woman like yourself could be a . . . I never guessed that you of all people . . . Oh have mercy on me!'

'What are you doing?' At the sound of the king's mighty roar the grovelling figure of the grand vizier spun around. 'Get away from her, you dog! How dare you throw yourself all over my wife!'

Xerxes could hardly contain himself.

'Guards!' he bellowed, and immediately several appeared.

Kneeling at the feet of the King. From a carving on an ancient obelisk.

'This man has gone too far! Take him away and I'll deal with him later – I don't know yet what punishment would suit him best.'

While two guards held the trembling Haman – to prevent his legs from collapsing beneath him – Harbonah, who had been serving at the banquet stepped forward.

'He knew well enough how to punish other people, Your Majesty.'

'What do you mean?' asked Xerxes, his eyes still on his ex-grand vizier.

'He got rid of anybody he didn't like. He even went as far as having a gallows built in his garden . . .'

'That's right . . .' chipped in Carkas, who had also been at table.

The king now turned to look at Harbonah, who continued '. . . he was going to use it to hang Mordecai, the man who saved Your Majesty's life.'

'. . . and it's twenty-two metres high!' Carkas added helpfully.

Esther gasped and Xerxes' face went purple.

'Mordecai?' he thundered. 'He was going to hang Mordecai? The man who saved my life? Take him out and hang him on his own gallows. Right now!'

The small group with the pathetic figure of Haman at the centre had turned to leave when Xerxes called them back. 'And take the ring of office from his finger! I want that seal back immediately. If it won't come off, cut it off!' he added impatiently.

'It was a mistake. Have mercy . . .' But Haman's feeble pleas fell on deaf ears. He was led out of the palace and executed on his own gallows. The proud selfish grand vizier minister was dead, and very few people were sorry.

'You are to have all his possessions,' said Xerxes turning to Esther. 'I made him rich and powerful, so whatever he had I now give to you.'

'Thank you, Your Majesty, I don't deserve such a great honour. However there is something else I think you should know . . .'

'And what's that, Cedar of Lebanon?' Xerxes sighed, certain that nothing could surprise him now.

'Mordecai, the man who once saved your life, is my cousin!'

The king merely raised his eyebrows. What a day this had turned out to be!

'Go and bring the Jew, Mordecai, to me,' he called to a guard. 'He's probably sitting near the palace gates . . .'

The guard soon returned with Mordecai, who was now wearing his old sack cloth again. He cast a puzzled glance from Esther to Xerxes, but said nothing.

'Enter, brave Mordecai!' enthused Xerxes. 'My beloved queen tells me you are her cousin. I have asked you here to tell you that you are my new grand vizier!'

Completely mystified, Mordecai bowed and accepted the ring that had once graced Haman's finger. Again he glanced at Esther, a question in his eyes.

'The king has found Haman to be an evil man,' she explained quickly. 'He has been sent to the gallows.'

'So now you will take over his job as grand vizier,' finished Xerxes.

He turned to smile at his wife, confident of her approval.

'This is all very well,' Mordecai interrupted, 'but the law still says that all Jews must die.'

Esther nodded. 'What are you going to do about that?'

'Don't worry, pomegranate!' the king soothed. 'You'll be alright! You and Mordecai will be living here in the safety of the palace. Now – I think I'll go to bed. It's been a long day and I didn't get much sleep last night.'

'But your Majesty . . .!'

Xerxes however had swept from the room, leaving a disturbed Esther and Mordecai behind him. True, their own safety was assured – but that wasn't enough!

As soon as she could, Esther spoke to the king again.

'Please, Xerxes, can't you alter that terrible decree?' she begged him.

Her husband stared at her in surprise.

'There's no need to worry,' he reassured her. 'I've already told you that you'll be safe. No harm will come to you.'

'I might be safe,' she answered, 'but my people aren't! Thousands of innocent men, women and children will die for no reason except that they are Jews!'

The king thought deeply, but shook his head.

'There's nothing I can do about it, beloved,' he said. 'An order, stamped with the king's seal must be carried out. Even I can't stop it!'

Esther stared at the floor in despair. She had failed! Even though her life, and her cousin's life, were not threatened her people were still doomed.

'I suppose there is one thing I could do . . .' Xerxes said suddenly.

'Yes? What's that?' Esther's face was bright and eager.

'I can issue another order which says that if any Jews are attacked then they have my permission to defend themselves and fight back. That way the people of Persia will realise that the first law was a mistake.'

Xerxes sat back, looking very pleased with himself. It wasn't exactly what she'd hoped for, Esther thought, but it would have to do! She ran from the room to find Mordecai, and soon the king's secretaries were writing out the new law. Again riders mounted their horses to take the order to all parts of the empire.

There was rejoicing amongst the Jews when they heard the king's command, for the news spread rapidly. Maybe they did have some hope after all!

The fateful day finally arrived. As Esther had expected, there was some fighting – but it wasn't the mass slaughter that Haman had planned, and hoped for, all those months before!

Instead of a time of mourning, the day became a festival, celebrated by Jews for generations to come. Every year on that day they would remember Queen Esther, and how her courage had saved them from destruction.

Through a hole in the roof

Stephen lay on his mat at home in Capernaum. It had been another long boring day, and he was feeling depressed and lonely. His mother and sisters had left the house at dawn to work in the fields, and they wouldn't be back until late that afternoon.

He'd slept a little, but mainly he had just lain awake, watching the shadows on the ceiling and thinking. Today, as on every day, his thoughts had returned to the day of his accident – when his life had tragically changed.

He had been an apprentice builder. The men who worked with him had often said he would do well – he was a 'natural' who listened carefully and learned quickly. He had enjoyed his trade and looked forward to the future – until the day he slipped and fell.

He still didn't know how it had happened. One moment he had been working on the roof and the next he was lying on his back, on the ground. He still didn't know how long he'd been unconscious. The first thing he remembered was one of his friends leaning over him with a worried look on his face.

'Are you in pain, Stephen?' he asked him.

'I can't feel anything,' Stephen had muttered, feeling dizzy. 'I . . . I can't move! I can't move!' He began to panic as the awful truth sank in. He couldn't move his body – from his neck down to his feet – he was paralysed!

His family was poor and couldn't afford a doctor, but everyone knew that a doctor couldn't help anyway. Stephen's injuries were too bad! He would have to spend the rest of his life lying on a mat. Useless – unable to do anything!

Every day the same thought went through his head: 'If only I had been more careful!' But he knew it was too late.

'I must have done something very bad and now I'm being punished for it,' he had once told his mother, but try as he might, he couldn't think of anything to deserve such a punishment. Why did it have to happen to him? All day these thoughts had gone round and round in his head, making him feel worse and worse, sadder and angrier.

Suddenly he heard voices and turned his head a little so that he could see the front door. His friends from work were just coming in, from the brilliant sunshine outside, into the cooler room.

'Are you there?' called a voice.

'What do you think?' Stephen growled. How could he be anywhere else?

His friends, grinning cheerfully, squatted in front of his mat so he could see them.

'What are you smiling about?' snapped Stephen.

All the loneliness and bitterness of the long day rushed out in angry words.

'It's all right for you lot! You can go anywhere you want; walk, climb, work. Me, I'm stuck here, day after day, by myself and what do you care?'

The friends stared in dismay at one another and then back to Stephen.

'We were only trying to cheer you up,' said Mark, a little offended.

'Well don't bother,' snapped Stephen.

'We've got some good news for you,' interrupted Paul.

'Yes,' John added. 'Jesus is back in Capernaum.'

'Jesus? Who's Jesus?' Stephen asked moodily.

'We've talked about him before,' explained Simon. 'He's the man who has performed miracles and healed people.'

'Yes, but has he healed someone who's paralysed?' grumbled Stephen. He didn't really want to sound so unpleasant, but he felt so fed up with himself, he couldn't control his angry words.

'We think he could . . . if he was given the chance,' said Mark.

Stephen stared at his friends in turn, as he considered what Mark had said.

'What are you getting at' he frowned finally.

'Well, we thought if we took you to Jesus and asked him nicely, he might cure you!' Paul looked very pleased with himself. 'That's why we're all here. We're going to carry you to him now . . .'

Stephen was silent. His anger and loneliness had melted away as he listened to his friends, and he wanted very much to believe what they were saying. They seemed so sure about this Jesus – but he didn't know. Was he such a special doctor that he could heal a paralysed man? He'd have to think . . .

Then, before he knew what was happening, his four friends had picked up a corner of the mat each and were carrying him out of the house!

'Hey!' Stephen cried. 'I haven't told you yet if I want to go!'

'You've got no choice,' grinned Mark.

Stephen screwed up his eyes as he was carried out into the dazzling sunshine. It had been so long since he had last left the house – partly because he was too heavy for his mother and sisters to carry, and partly because he had always felt ashamed. It was so humiliating having to be dressed and fed like a baby . . .

Simon moved so that his shadow fell across Stephen's face, shielding him from the sun's rays.

'Thanks,' muttered Stephen, opening his eyes.

Several people stopped and stared at the strange procession making its way along the street. A little girl skipped alongside them for a while and then asked shyly,

'What are you doing?'

'Haven't you ever seen a paralysed man going for a walk before?' answered Paul.

The little girl stopped to think about this, then shrugged her shoulders and skipped off in the opposite direction.

'Where is this Jesus?' Stephen asked curiously. It seemed that his friends knew where they were going.

'I heard he was staying at his friend Peter's house,' John replied. 'It's just around this corner, we'll be there in a minute or two.'

The four friends didn't say much, so Stephen lay on his mat thinking. It was a hot day and he could hear them breathing heavily as they carried him along the road. He watched Simon and Paul's faces. They seemed so sure this man Jesus could cure him. Well, if they believed in him, then . . .

'Oh no!'

His thoughts were interrupted as his carriers came to a sudden halt. John groaned.

'What's wrong? What's happening?' Stephen tried to twist his head to see, but couldn't.

'There are hundreds of people here,' Simon told him. 'They're crowding outside the house, so the inside must be full as well.'

'How are we going to get through?' wondered John.

'We'll just have to push our way,' said Mark decidedly. 'I never thought there'd be so many people here! I hoped we'd be the only ones . . .'

Stephen lay quietly as his friends struggled off again. He could hear people moving and whispering as they neared the house. There must be a huge crowd!

'Excuse us,' said Mark, trying to shoulder his way through the throng of people. 'We have a man here on a mat and we want to take him to Jesus to be healed.'

'Well you should have got here earlier,' retorted the man he attempted to push past. 'My wife and I have been waiting since dawn. Susanna thinks that this Jesus is the only person who can do anything for her corns . . .'

Mark pushed against him again, his face pink with indignation. Corns indeed! His poor friend Stephen's life had been ruined by the accident, and this woman was worrying about her corns!

But it was no use. Even when the four friends managed to drag Stephen forward a little way they soon came to up against another solid mass of people.

'You won't get in there,' said an old woman who was squashed near the doorway. 'They're jammed in there so tight no one can move! Everyone in Capernaum has come to hear Jesus teach . . .'

Simon, who was the tallest, craned his head over her shoulder. She was obviously right, and he turned back to his companions glumly.

'It's no use – we'll never get him in. We might as well go home . . .'

Sadly they backed out the way they had come.

'I wish they'd make up their minds,' grumbled the woman with the corns to her husband. Simon wished that he had stepped on her foot.

Stephen's heart sank. He supposed he had been silly to let them raise his hopes, just to have them dashed. All his bitterness and sorrow welled up again inside him, and tears came into his eyes. Why him? Why did he have to fall off the roof, and why was he now being stopped from getting help?

'We could wait until they've all gone home,' suggested Paul, tentatively. 'It will be sunset in a couple of hours . . .'

'They could stay here for ages!' Mark spoke tersely, his words betraying the worry in his eyes. 'We don't know where Jesus is planning to go tomorrow – there's got to be another way!'

'Well, let's go and think,' suggested Simon. He was a slow, rather quiet person, who always liked to plan things carefully.

They carried Stephen to a nearby tree and placed him in the shade, making sure there weren't any stones under him first. This was important, because as Stephen wouldn't be able to feel them, he could end up with nasty wounds on his back.

'I'll stay with Stephen,' Simon decided, so the other three hurried back towards the house.

Simon sat beside his friend but said nothing. Both men were disappointed, and so what was there to say? After a few minutes the others returned, shaking their heads.

'There are just too many people,' John informed them. 'It's impossible – we'll never get through.'

They all had the same thought – they would have to go home, just as soon as Mark came back.

'Here he comes!' John pointed at the approaching figure. 'He looks excited – I wonder if he's thought of something!'

At that moment, Mark ran up to his friends, panting heavily and grinning from ear to ear.

'I've found a way we can get into the house,' he blurted.

'How?' asked John amazed. 'We searched and searched and we couldn't . . .'

'We can get through the roof!' Mark interrupted excitedly.

'What?' chorused four voices.

'We can go up the outside stairs, make a hole in the roof and lower Stephen on his mat right down in front of Jesus!'

Everyone stared at Mark in amazement. Had the heat affected his brain?

'I don't think Peter will think kindly of people who make holes in his roof . . .' began John doubtfully.

'Don't be silly!' scoffed Mark. 'We're builders aren't we? If we can build a roof then surely we can pull one apart and fix it afterwards!'

The others nodded in agreement, but Stephen wasn't so sure about swinging through the air on his mat.

'I don't think this is such a good idea,' he faltered. 'I've already had one nasty fall . . .'

Simon chose to ignore his protests.

'Right, let's do it,' he decided, grabbing one corner of the mat.

So once again Stephen was carried towards the house, however this time they headed around the back towards the stairs. No one noticed them struggling up them with their precious load . . .

Stephen lay silently, his heart beating faster and faster as they climbed. Memories of the last time he was on a roof flooded back, and he felt more and more uneasy. But his friends had lifted many loads up onto buildings, and soon he found himself lying safely on the roof of the house.

'I think we should start the hole here,' advised John, moving carefully towards the centre. 'I can hear a voice directly under me.'

The others agreed and soon they were hard at work, pulling the branches and mud away to make a hole. As it grew larger, Paul noticed a smile on Simon's face.

'What are you grinning about?' he whispered.

'I was just wondering what the people below us might be thinking about being sprayed with pieces of dried mud!' he replied.

Paul grinned as well as he poked his face through the hole. A few faces looked up but quickly turned back to the man who was speaking. Some people would put up with anything to hear Jesus, Paul thought. He wondered if Peter knew what was happening to his roof.

As Simon, Paul and John worked steadily, Mark slipped away and returned soon after with some lengths of rope. Skilfully he tied them to the four corners of Stephen's mat, checking the knots were tight and secure.

Stephen lay and listened to all the activity. As the minutes passed, he became more and more excited, and impatient. Would they never be ready?

'I think the hole's big enough,' Simon announced.

The others crawled over to Stephen's mat and grabbed the ropes, checking again that they wouldn't come away from the mat. They didn't want Stephen to fall off halfway down!

Neither did Stephen! His heart pounded as the mat was positioned over the gaping hole.

'Wait a moment! I've changed my . . .'

But it was too late! He was already swinging through the air. Memories of his fall came flooding back to him and his head spun with fear. He clenched his teeth and closed his eyes tightly, while above him his friends slowly and carefully fed the ropes through their strong hands. Very gently the mat was lowered to the floor . . .

'Are these ropes long enough?' whispered Paul, sweating heavily.

'I hope so!' Mark looked at the coil still lying curled on the roof top. 'It was difficult to judge . . .'

In the room below, the scene had changed dramatically. Jesus had been speaking, but now he stopped and his eyes followed everyone else's up towards the roof. The crowd gave a gasp of astonishment as Stephen came into sight . . .

The four friends kept letting out the ropes, and the mat came down lower and lower. Everybody had to squeeze up even tighter to get out of its way! Eventually it reached the floor and Stephen, resting at the feet of Jesus, breathed a huge sigh of relief. He was glad that that was over!

A buzz passed around the room. Several people untied the ropes and the four friends hauled them up. What was going to happen now? Everyone wondered. Exciting things usually happened when Jesus was around!

Jesus stared up silently at the four expectant faces peering around the edges of the hole. He could see how much they wanted him to help their friend, and he knew they believed he could do it. He smiled, lowering his face to look at Stephen. A great hush came over the room.

'My son . . .' His voice was gentle, the expression in his eyes infinitely caring. 'Your sins are forgiven!'

The words were spoken clearly for all to hear.

The room buzzed again with voices, and almost immediately Jesus spun around and pointed to some men sitting in a corner. His eyes, which had seemed so gentle a moment ago, now flashed with anger.

'I know what you're thinking!' he shouted. 'Why don't you say it out loud?'

Everyone turned, trying to see who had made Jesus so angry.

'He must mean those Pharisees over there!' they whispered to each other. 'But how does he know what they're thinking?'

In their corner, the Pharisees sat defiantly, declining to answer. Jesus' voice rang out again.

'Then I'll tell everybody instead! You thought, 'Who does he think he is, talking like this? No one but God can forgive sins.'

The Pharisees shuffled their feet in embarrassment and stared at the floor. Jesus was right – that was what they had been thinking. How did he know what was in their minds?

'It's true, isn't it?' Jesus demanded. 'Well, let me ask you another question. Is it easier to say to this paralysed man 'Your sins are forgiven', or to say, 'Get up, pick up your mat and walk?'

The room was tense with excitement as the Pharisees still refused to answer him. The crowd pressed forward. They knew something dramatic was about to happen and no one wanted to miss a thing!

Stephen, too, lay and waited. He was bewildered and confused, for this was not what he had imagined would happen. He didn't know what to think, and there was certainly nothing he could do . . .

Then Jesus turned back to him and held out his hand.

'I'll show you that I can forgive sins,' he told the helpless figure. 'I want you to get up, pick up your mat and walk home.'

For one dreadful moment, Stephen thought nothing was going to happen. Then he suddenly felt a surge of power rush through his body! He could feel the blood pumping through his chest, arms and legs – and then he could feel the hard dirt floor! It dug into him, and Stephen thought no pain had ever felt as sweet! He raised himself onto his elbows, and then struggled to a sitting position. There was a soft gasp from the assembled people, and then, before he knew it, Stephen was on his feet!

Stephen still looked dazed as he made his way out of the room, through the tiny passage the people had made for him. He stumbled out into the sunshine, where he was mobbed by the crowd who touched him and plied him with questions. His eyes were half blinded by tears of joy.

'Oh, thank you – thank you Jesus! It's so good to be alive!' he shouted, throwing down the mat he had grown to hate so deeply. He glanced around him in confusion, still overcome with amazement. 'Please – let me through – I must go and find my friends!'

Up on the roof, Mark, John, Paul and Simon were over-joyed too. They laughed and cried and hugged one another.

'He did it!' Paul yelled delightedly 'We knew Jesus could cure him all along!'

They grinned down through the hole and waved to Jesus. Their happy faces were full of gratitude and Jesus smiled at them as he waved back.

'What a wonderful day!' exclaimed Simon. 'Let's go and find Stephen – he must be so excited.'

'Yes, let's!' echoed Paul, and the four friends headed for the stairs.

'Hey – wait a minute,' called Mark, stopping suddenly. The others turned to look at him.

'What's wrong?' Simon asked.

Mark looked at his friends and grinned widely. 'Haven't you forgotten something?' he chided.

'First we've got to fix the roof!'

The healing touch

Lydia had been working hard all morning. With a deep sigh she put her broom away and glanced around the room. She smiled, for at last her house was clean, neat and tidy. The hours of sweeping, dusting and scrubbing had been well spent. She had planned to do some baking that afternoon, but now, feeling hot and weary, she decided to sit down in her kitchen and put her feet up for a while.

But just as she was getting comfortable, Lydia heard a knock. Wearily she rose to her feet and headed for the door.

'Hello, Lydia. Can I come in for a few minutes?' Lydia's friend, Sarah, stood blinking in the midday sun, looking hot and unhappy. She sounded very tired.

'Of course,' replied Lydia, opening the door wider. Thankfully, Sarah stepped into the shady house and went into the kitchen.

Lydia prepared two cool drinks and placed them on the table. Her own tiredness was forgotten as she looked at Sarah, for she could tell that something was very wrong . . .

Sarah sipped at her drink slowly. At last she spoke.

'I saw that new doctor in the next town this morning,' she said, playing nervously with her cup.

'And?' Lydia prompted, sensing immediately that Sarah's news was not good.

Sarah stopped fiddling with her cup and looked up at her friend.

'And it's no use,' she sniffed miserably. 'He was no help at all!'

Tears appeared in her eyes, and Lydia grasped her friend's hands, trying to reassure her.

'Don't you feel even a little bit better?' she asked hopefully.

Sarah shook her head. 'No, not at all. I've had this wretched illness for twelve years – twelve long years! I've seen every single doctor I know and I'm still no better!'

Lydia was silent. She knew all about her friend's problem

and couldn't think of any way to help her.

'I've spent all my money on doctors!,' Sarah wailed, wiping her nose on her handkerchief. 'Some of their so-called cures are just nonsense! I do believe I feel worse now than I did before I started!'

Her head drooped again and there was silence in the room. Lydia felt helpless. She had tried hard to help Sarah, and every time she'd heard of a new doctor or cure, she'd told her friend who had gone away with new hope. But each time Sarah returned with the same story – the doctors could not cure her illness.

'There is no one else to go to,' she sobbed. 'I've got hardly any money now anyway! There's no hope left at all . . .'

As Sarah continued to weep helplessly, Lydia was suddenly reminded of something she had heard earlier that morning. When she had gone to the well to fetch her water, she'd overheard some of the women talking. But dare she mention what they had said to Sarah? Was it fair to keep on trying to raise her hopes?'

I don't know if this will help . . .' Lydia hesitated.

Sarah played with her cup,and her friend could tell she wasn't really listening. Everything was useless – nobody could help . . .

Lydia drew a deep breath and continued.

'I heard some women talking at the well this morning about a blind man.'

'What about him?' asked Sarah dully. She wasn't really interested in anyone else's problems – she had enough of her own! And what did a blind man have to do with her illness anyway? She wasn't blind!

'They said that he can now see,' continued Lydia. 'He was cured by a man called Jesus . . .'

'Jesus?' There was a small spark of interest in Sarah's voice. She thought for a moment. 'I haven't heard of a doctor called Jesus . . .'

'Oh – he's not a doctor!' explained Lydia. 'The women told me that he was walking along the road with his friends when they passed a blind man, sitting under a tree. When the blind man heard who it was that was passing, he called out and asked Jesus to cure him.'

'And . . .?' asked Sarah.

'And Jesus touched his eyes with his hand and instantly the man could see!'

Sarah was astonished. 'What – he cured a man's blindness by just touching him? I don't believe it!'

'I didn't either, at first,' agreed Lydia, 'but the women all insisted it was true. And he's cured other people as well . . .'

Sarah sat deep in thought. 'And you say he's not a doctor?' she frowned.

Lydia shook her head. 'No – but he must have some very special powers!'

Sarah wriggled in her chair nervously, twisting her handkerchief between her hands.

'Do you think . . .?' she began, and then turned away unhappily.

'Do I think that he could cure you?' Lydia finished Sarah's question. She shrugged. 'What have you got to lose?'

She hadn't meant to build up her friend's hopes again, but she could sense she was becoming excited. If the women at the well thought that this man Jesus was special . . .

'We could go out this afternoon and find him!'

'How do we do that?' asked Sarah doubtfully. 'He could be anywhere! It would be impossible to find one man walking around the country with his friends. We don't even know what he looks like.'

'The women said he's often surrounded by crowds, so it shouldn't be too difficult,' Lydia returned. 'And when we do, you can just go up to him, tell him what's wrong and ask if he . . .'

'No!' cried Sarah sharply. The keen look disappeared from her face in an instant.

Lydia sat upright in her chair. 'No?' she exclaimed.

'No,' Sarah repeated, firmly. 'I can't go up to a man I don't know and talk to him about my problem in front of a crowd of people! It would just be too embarrassing.' She shook her head sadly. 'No, I couldn't do it.'

They fell silent again, their hopes dashed. Lydia understood. Sarah's illness was very personal, not the sort of thing you could tell a man who was a total stranger. He might be shocked – and she would feel so ashamed! And especially in front of a crowd of people!

'Perhaps I could talk to him when no one was around?' she suggested, her voice a little hopeful.

Lydia shook her head sadly. 'I don't think he's ever alone. The women said he is very popular and always has people following him.'

'Oh,' Sarah's head drooped again. Lydia wished she hadn't mentioned it at all. She had raised her friend's hopes for nothing. Why hadn't she kept quiet? And yet . . .

'There must be a way,' she thought out loud. 'This Jesus is supposed to have such great power of healing. There must be some way you can see him . . .'

Sarah's fingers drummed on the table. She spoke hesitantly.

'If he's so powerful . . . I wonder . . .? If I just touched his clothes . . . do you think that might be enough to cure me?'

Her eyes brightened at the idea. 'Then I wouldn't have to explain anything at all!'

She smiled broadly at her friend, her excitement rising again.

'That's what I'll do! I'll just slip through the crowd and when no one is looking, I'll touch his clothes. Nothing could be easier!'

Once again she was hopeful that her long illness was nearly over.

'Will you come with me?' Sarah asked her friend shyly. 'I would feel braver if you were there.'

Lydia smiled, her tiredness and baking plans forgotten.

'Of course,' she said. 'We'll go out this afternoon.'

The two friends ate a hasty meal before hurrying out into the hot afternoon sun, in search of Jesus. They asked everyone they met if they had seen him, but the people shook their heads. No, they hadn't seen the man who always had crowds following him!

By mid afternoon, the two friends' hopes had begun to fade. It was so hot – and so very disappointing! This man Jesus could be the answer to Sarah's problem – if only they could find him! Someone must know where he was!

They were trudging along the dusty road when suddenly Lydia cried out, pointing ahead of them.

'There – up ahead! There's a crowd of people! I wonder if that's Jesus? Oh, please let it be him . . .'

They hurried towards the people, Sarah's hopes rising again. But as she came closer to the crowd her heart began to pound, and she slowed down, almost stopping.

'I . . . I don't think I'll bother,' she whispered to Lydia. 'It wasn't really such a good idea . . .'

But Lydia grabbed her by the arm and pulled her along. 'Come on,' she urged. 'You've come this far. You must try!'

Sarah's knees were trembling. 'I'm scared,' she faltered. Her voice was shaking as well.

'I know,' sympathised Lydia. 'I know . . .'

Sarah looked at her friend and then back at the crowd, trying to re-assure herself. She thought again of her plan – it was easy, nothing could go wrong! No one would even notice her and she did want to be well again!

'All right,' she nodded, taking a deep breath. 'Wish me luck – here I go!'

Lydia squeezed her hand and watched as Sarah made her way through the crowd, gradually pushing closer and closer to the man who was the centre of attention. Lydia caught glimpses of him now and then. Was this the man who had power to heal? She stood on tiptoe and waited and watched.

Sarah's determination began to waver again as she wove in and out of the jostling crowd. She felt as though everyone was watching her and had guessed exactly what she was planning. Deep down, however, she knew these thoughts were silly. No one was paying any attention to her – they were either talking among themselves or listening to Jesus. They took no notice of the woman who carefully put out her hand and touched the hem of Jesus' robe . . .

As soon as her hand brushed against the garment, Sarah felt a tremendous surge of power sweep right through her body. She shuddered as the strange tingling passed over her, from her head down to the soles of her feet, and then drew in her breath sharply. Her whole body felt different – it felt re-born! In an instant, Sarah knew that her illness had left her – that she had been healed. She didn't need to go home and wait like the doctors had advised her, and she knew she would never have to try another pill or potion. She was cured – and Jesus the healer had not even had to look at her! Sarah stood there stunned, her mind full of wonder, gazing at the man who had cured her, marvelling at the power he must have.

But as Sarah stood behind him, a sudden change seemed to come over Jesus. He stopped what he was saying in mid-sentence, frowning slightly as he swung around.

'Who touched me?' he demanded.

His friends were surprised. They looked at one another and then at Jesus.

'Who touched you?' one asked. 'What do you mean, Rabbi? There are so many people here, any one of them could have accidentally pushed against you!'

Jesus ignored his words. 'Who touched me?' he repeated, more insistently still. The people near to him looked puzzled, and his disciples glanced at one another nervously. Perhaps someone had bumped into him or trodden on his foot!

As Jesus gazed around, the crowd became quiet. Some of the people shuffled their feet, guiltily.

'Was it you?' whispered one to another, trying to find someone to blame. 'It must have been – it certainly wasn't me!'

Sarah stood like a statue, wishing the ground would open and swallow her up! She knew exactly what Jesus was talking about; he must have felt the surge of power leave him as she had touched the hem of his robe! How she wished everybody would start talking again and let her slip quietly away! But Jesus just stood there waiting . . .

As she stood there, her heart beating desperately, Sarah began to understand what had happened. She was indeed well – she had been healed by this man's power. But she hadn't asked him! Now Jesus wanted to know who had touched him, and Sarah knew she would have to own up!

Blushing deeply she inched forward and fell at his feet.

'It was me, Master!' she whispered, her eyes lowered in shame. 'I was the one who touched your clothes . . .'

Murmurs of surprise were followed by a hush as the crowd waited and wondered. What would happen now?

Sarah kept her head bowed as she told her story to Jesus. She told him everything – all about her long illness, about the doctors who had not been able to cure her, and how she had been too ashamed to speak to him and had decided to just touch him instead . . .

'You were my only hope,' she concluded, her voice trembling. 'And your power has made me well . . .'

The crowd waited silently to see what Jesus would do.

Sarah was glad that her ordeal was over. She looked up at Jesus' face as she finished her story, and when she saw the love and understanding in his eyes she stopped trembling and gave a tentative smile. Jesus wasn't angry with her! Instead, he returned her shy smile with one of his own, a smile so full of understanding and love that Sarah felt a strange tingling surge through her body again. He held out his hand and gently helped her to her feet.

'It is your faith that has made you well,' he told her quietly, holding her hand. 'Now go home in peace – be healed of your trouble!'

He smiled again at her and Sarah positively beamed with happiness! Her heart felt as if it was bursting with gratitude and relief.

'Oh, thank you, Master – thank you!' she cried joyfully.

Jesus squeezed her hand once more before he turned and continued on his way. The people followed him, chattering excitedly amongst themselves about what they had just seen and heard. They jostled past Sarah, who still hadn't moved. Her eyes were fixed on Jesus, and she didn't notice the curious stares of the crowd or hear their comments as they passed her. Before long she was alone in the middle of the dusty road. The people were now some distance away and Jesus had disappeared from view.

'Sarah – Oh, Sarah! How wonderful!'

Sarah turned as she heard Lydia's voice. She came hurrying towards her friend, and the two women hugged one another joyfully, tears of happiness flowing down their cheeks. As Sarah clung to Lydia, she told her of the words which Jesus had spoken, and the look of love and understanding she had seen in his eyes. As long as she lived, Sarah would never forget this wonderful day – the day when Jesus the healer had made her well again!

'I've so much to do!'

Another day was drawing to a close. The sun, which had been blazing since morning, was now low in the western sky. Mary wandered out of her house and stood gazing at the vivid oranges and reds of the sunset. As the fiery ball disappeared below the horizon, the evening air began to feel pleasant and cool. This was the time of day Mary liked best and she leaned against the doorpost, breathing deeply.

Her eyes wandered lazily from the painted sky to rest on a group of people walking slowly along the road. As she gazed, she suddenly straightened, recognising one of the figures. With an exclamation of joy she turned and ran quickly into the house, calling loudly to her sister.

'Martha! Martha – come quickly!'

Martha ran from the kitchen wiping her hands on a towel.

'What's wrong, Mary?' she asked anxiously. 'Are you hurt?'

Mary laughed as she grabbed her sister by the arm and pulled her towards the front door.

'I'm sorry if I frightened you, Martha,' she apologised. 'And no, there's nothing wrong with me. But look who's coming down the road!'

By now they were outside the house and Mary pointed into the distance. Martha squinted as she followed her sister's finger.

'I don't know who . . .' she began, puzzled. Then her face lit up.

'It's Jesus,' she exclaimed delightedly as she recognised the approaching figures. 'I didn't know he was in Bethany at the moment!'

Mary shook her head, her eyes still fixed in the distance.

'Neither did I,' she answered, 'but what a lovely surprise!'

The approaching group had grown smaller now because some of the men had gone to their homes.

'If Jesus has been teaching all day he is bound to be

hungry,' decided Mary. 'I know – let's ask him to come an have dinner!'

'I was just about to suggest the same thing,' nodde Martha. 'Oh!'

She stopped abruptly and turned to glance into the house.

'Everything's in a mess . . . I wasn't expecting visitor today! Whatever will Jesus think?'

Mary shrugged her shoulders. 'I don't think Jesus wi care,' she laughed. 'He'll probably be so tired he won't eve notice. You know what it's like when he's teaching – ther are so many people and he doesn't get a chance to eat ver much. He'll just want to sit down and relax . . .'

'But the floor – it needs sweeping! And the cushions ar crooked and the curtains could do with a wash! Oh – and haven't been to the market today! There won't be anythin special for him to eat!'

Martha ran inside, fussing. Frantically. she bega straightening cushions, shifting furniture and picking u invisible pieces of fluff off the carpets.

'Don't be silly, Martha!' Mary called, trying hard to concea her irritation.

'The house is always spotless – you never let it get untidy If we don't hurry out now and catch him he'll be gone. Look he's almost here already! Do you want me to go alone, or ar you coming with me?'

As she spoke, Mary waved to Jesus who had already seer her standing near her front door. As he headed towards he he waved back. The last two men with him also waved t Mary, then said goodbye to Jesus and continued on thei way.

Mary stepped forward, only to be knocked aside by he sister, who rushed out of the house like a whirlwind and se off up the street, tidying her hair as she ran. When sh reached Jesus she was almost too puffed out to speak!

'Jesus,' she panted, as she hurried up to him. 'It's s wonderful to see you again! You must come and stay with us have a meal and . . .'

Jesus smiled down into Martha's pink face, and passed weary hand through his hair.

'Thank you, Martha,' he replied. 'I was hoping you'd as me. It's been a very busy day and I'd really like to sit dow and relax in the peace and quiet of your home. I can think o nothing better!'

Martha was delighted. She flushed even pinker at his words and led the way towards the house where Mary was still waiting at the door.

'You must excuse the mess the house is in,' Martha fussed over her shoulder. 'I wasn't expecting visitors today! Of course – you know you are always welcome here any time. It won't take long to tidy up and I won't disturb you . . .'

Jesus turned from the busy little figure to smile at Mary. He held her hand tightly as they entered the house.

'Hello, Mary. How lovely it is to see you again!'

He glanced around the room and laughed. 'Martha, I should have known! The house is as spotless as ever! I thought you were teasing me when you said it was untidy but . . .'

But Martha's voice, as it floated from the kitchen was serious.

'You know I never joke about such things, Lord! I'm ashamed of it – but don't worry, I'll soon clear things up. Sit down and I'll get you a drink. You must be very thirsty . . .'

Jesus glanced at Mary who shrugged her shoulders.

'You know what Martha's like,' she whispered. 'Even after she's cleaned and dusted and swept she can always find some fault with her own housework.'

Jesus nodded, and threw himself thankfully onto a soft comfy couch. He kicked off his sandals and sighed with pleasure.

'Ah, that feels good! Those roads are so stony and my feet are very sore. Hasn't it been hot today?'

Without waiting for an answer he closed his eyes and wriggled further down into the couch to make himself more comfortable. He knew he was in a home where he could relax, away from everyone else, and he lay back to enjoy the peace and quiet. Mary silently curled up on the floor near him, tucking her legs underneath her in a comfortable position. She was happy to be near the teacher she loved, and content to see him so peaceful. Nothing disturbed the quiet and stillness in the room . . .'

'Now, here we are, here's a nice cool drink! Just what you need . . .'

Both Mary and Jesus jumped as Martha's sudden voice disturbed the silence. She lay the tray on a table.

A tiny groan rose from Jesus' throat as he slowly opened his eyes. He took the drink from Martha who was smiling broadly, unaware that anything was wrong.

'That will make you feel better,' she continued, pumping up the cushions behind him more comfortably. She wiped the side-table down carefully before re-arranging the tray.

'Here's your drink, Mary.'

Mary glanced up, noticing there were only two cups. Her brows furrowed in surprise.

'Where's your drink Martha? Aren't you going to sit down and join us?'

Martha grunted as she bustled out of the room.

'I haven't got time to sit down and have a drink!' she remarked, looking at her sister meaningfully. 'There's too much to do!'

Mary sighed, as from the kitchen came the clink and clatter of bowls and spoons, telling them that a meal was being prepared.

'But Martha . . .' Jesus called, but she didn't hear him. He finished his drink and placed the cup near him on the floor. Mary thought he still looked very tired. She felt that what he needed was a long sleep.

'That drink was very welcome,' he said and nestled back amongst the cushions on the couch. He didn't close his eyes but looked down at Mary who was still sipping at her drink.

'Tell me what you've been doing, Mary,' he said gently.

'I'd rather hear what you've been doing, Lord,' she smiled. 'Tell me about the people you've met and the stories you've told since we last saw you.'

'Well . . .'

But Jesus had hardly begun to speak when Martha came bustling back into the room. They waited patiently as she arranged the rugs beneath Jesus' feet and re-arranged the other cushions in the room. She brushed some dust from the table and picked up a piece of fluff from the floor.

'Excuse me,' she said sharply to her sister as she moved Mary to make sure there weren't any other pieces of fluff she might have missed. Mary looked pained as she shifted but said nothing.

Suddenly Martha stopped and sniffed loudly. They all turned their heads to the kitchen where the smell of burning was coming from.

'Oh no!' Martha exclaimed and rushed back into the kitchen. More banging, clattering and muttering followed.

Mary didn't seem at all troubled by her sister's worries and calmly turned back to Jesus.

'You were going to tell me about your day,' she reminded him.

Jesus glanced towards the kitchen with a frown on his face, but then relaxed and began to talk.

'I told a story the other day about a woman who had lost a coin,' he began.

Mary shifted into a more comfortable position and leaned against the couch.

'Tell me,' she said expectantly.

Her eyes never left Jesus' face as he spoke softly. The noise Martha was making faded into the background as she listened to his words. He told wonderful stories and this one was new to her. She loved to listen to him and was sorry she couldn't always be with him on his journeys. Mary, her sister and their brother Lazarus often gave him money so he could buy food while he was away – but to Mary it wasn't the same. Now she had him all to herself – she could listen and ask as many questions as she liked. This was a very special time for her.

Jesus halted as a sudden crash sounded from the kitchen.

'Oh no, now look what's happened!' Martha's voice was distraught. 'Everything is going wrong today!'

She stamped to the door and glared at Mary, her wet hand on her hips. Mary glanced at her sister for a moment and the turned back to Jesus. Martha continued to glower at h sister, but it made no difference, Mary took no notice of h at all. She was too interested in what Jesus was saying.

'The meal will be ready soon,' Martha stated loudly.

'Don't go to any special trouble Martha,' Jesus soothed hearing the annoyance in her voice. 'If you're not having good day then come and sit down here for a while, and hav a rest . . .'

'I can't!,' Martha responded, horrified. 'I have the meal prepare! We'd never eat if I sat around in here all the time. C course, if I had some help, I . . .'

But the hint fell on deaf ears. If Mary had heard she didn take any notice.

'It's going to be a special meal,' Martha added important 'That's why it's taking so long.'

'But I don't want a special meal!' Jesus told he 'Something simple is all I need. I'd much rather we all s here in the quiet together. Don't go to a lot of trouble for m please Martha!'

'No, no, it's no trouble!' cried Martha. 'You've had a lon day and you need to eat some good food. You probabl haven't eaten properly for days! Never let it be said that yo don't get a decent meal in my house! I know it's taking while – but I'd have had it ready sooner if I didn't have to d it all by myself. It's much quicker when two are workin instead of just the one . . .'

Again her words were aimed at Mary, and again Mar ignored them. Martha returned to the kitchen, grumblin under her breath.

Jesus shook his head sadly as he heard Martha bang th door. Then he continued to tell Mary about the people he ha met recently. He told her about a man who was blind bu who could now see, and a woman who could now walk. H also told her some of the questions he had been asked tha day and the answers he had given.

A great crash followed by a cry from the kitchen made the both jump. Martha rushed back into the room with flou spattered all down the front of her robe. In her hands was bowl that was now in three pieces.

'Now look what's happened!' she exploded. 'My best bow is broken, there's flour everywhere and we still haven anything to eat! I'll have to start all over again and it's all her fault!'

She pointed angrily at Mary who sat up in surprise.

'Me?' she exclaimed. 'How can it be my fault? I haven't done anything! I've been in here all the time.'

'That's exactly what I mean,' retorted Martha, her eyes flashing angrily. 'If you had helped me in the kitchen this wouldn't have happened! Why should I be expected to do all the work?'

She turned to face Jesus.

'Rabbi, please tell my sister to help me! She'll listen to you! I've got so much to do and I can't finish it by myself . . .'

'Martha . . . Martha!' soothed Jesus. 'Don't upset yourself! I told you I only wanted something simple to eat. There's no need . . .'

'Of course there's a need to make something special for you!' Martha interrupted. 'But I can't do it all by myself! And all the time Mary just sits there doing nothing . . .'

'You are a wonderful cook, Martha,' Jesus continued. 'And it's a well-known fact that anything you prepare is delicious! But you mustn't get so upset about little things. You say Mary has been doing nothing, but that isn't true.' He held up his hand for silence as Martha tried to interrupt again. 'Mary has been listening to the stories I've been telling, and it's important for her to hear them. In fact, it's important for you to hear them as well . . .'

'I would sit down and listen if I had the time,' replied Martha tartly. 'But I have my work to do first.'

'What I have to say is far more important than housework or cooking,' responded Jesus. He looked into Martha's eyes, and she lowered them slightly.

'You can do that any time! But I'm not here all the time, am I?'

Martha shook her head. 'But that's why . . .'

'Mary has chosen the right thing to do tonight, and I'm not going to criticise her!'

The three looked at one another in silence for some time, and then Martha turned and went back into her kitchen, her head in a whirl. She had only tried to do the right thing in giving Jesus a good meal!

She thought hard as she carefully lifted her rolls out of the oven. Perhaps what he'd said was true! They hadn't seen very much of him lately – there was always a crowd around Jesus, and the disciples were sometimes disgruntled if their

leader spent his time talking to women. And now, when I
was here and they had him all to themselves she'd been to
busy in the kitchen to spend any time with him! The fan
dish that she had been preparing would have looke
impressive – but perhaps it would have been more sensib
to have settled for a plainer one that was quicker to make .

Martha smiled as she set the hot rolls onto a platter. Sh
arranged some fruit beside them and added some rour
slabs of cheese. It looked very appetising, she thought – ar
that was all there was to prepare! In a few moments she to
would be able to sit at Jesus' feet with her sister and listen
his stories.

She threw off her apron, eager now to join the others. Sh
no longer felt tired and harrassed – everything was so mud
easier when Jesus was around!

With a light heart, Martha picked up the supper tray ar
strode out of the kitchen . . .

By the pool

Adam lay helplessly listening to the bubble and gurgle of the water. He turned his head away from the pool as a woman on the other side jumped in, not caring if the healing waters cured her of her illness. He wasn't interested . . .

So many people had come to the Pool of Bethzatha since Adam had first arrived there! At first it had been terribly exciting. So many other sufferers were made well again that it seemed to the sick man that it was only a matter of time before he himself was healed. But as the weeks became months, and the months became years, Adam came to realise how impossible his situation was.

How long was it he had lain there? The number thirty-eight came to mind. Whether it was thirty-eight years or not, Adam knew it had been a dreadfully long time! Too many years for him to want to remember, that was certain!

His thoughts returned to the days when he first arrived at the Pool of Bethzatha. He had been told it was special. Some thought it was an angel who came down and moved the waters; others said it was a spring that bubbled up at times, but whatever it was, it gave results. Everyone knew that whoever entered the pool first when the waters moved would be healed of their sickness. But – and this was where Adam's problem lay – it was only the first person into the water who was ever cured! And poor Adam was never quick enough . . .

The friends who had brought him here had been very kind at first, sitting with him day after day and watching the waters. But no one ever knew when the movement would begin! It happened at odd times, which meant the sick had to be constantly on guard, and after a while Adam's friends decided they couldn't always stay with him. They had their own lives to lead, their own families to attend to, and one by one over the years they had gradually drifted away . . .

'We'll come back tomorrow,' they had promised. But that

night would be the night when the waters bubbled upwards, and next morning Adam could only tell them another chance had been missed. Then his friends had become disheartened, and eventually none of them came any more. Now Adam was completely alone . . .

That had been years ago and Adam now knew he had no hope. People were kind enough and shared their food with him, but he knew deep down he would spend the rest of his life by this pool.

He glanced around. On every side he was surrounded by the sick, lame and blind; they had all heard of the pool's healing powers and had come in hope of a cure. He had seen many arrive – and many go! If only one of them could have been him! Now he was alone and friendless – how different he had imagined his life would be!

At that moment a shadow passed across him, and Adam's thoughts were jolted back to the present. He opened his eyes, shielding them with his hand against the bright rays of the sun. Above him a figure stood, watching him.

'I hear you have been crippled for a long time . . .' the voice was gentle but had a quiet authority which made Adam strain his eyes harder. It was so rare for anyone to show any interest in his complaint!

'I think it's been about thirty-eight years.'

The stranger looked into his eyes and Adam gazed back, mesmerised by the depth of understanding in them . . .

'Do you want to get better?' he asked gently.

Adam nodded dumbly, ashamed for a moment as he felt tears springing into his eyes. Did he want to get better? Why else would he be lying beside this pool? Of course he wanted to be cured! Wasn't that what he wished for every hour of every day? He didn't want to be a cripple!

He was silent for a few seconds as he composed his thoughts, then he swallowed once or twice and answered.

'Of course I want to get well.' His voice was a little shaky 'But I can't do it on my own – I need someone to help me into the pool when the water is stirred. When I try by myself, someone always gets there first and my chance is gone.'

The stranger nodded as if he understood. Then he smiled at Adam kindly.

'You don't need to enter the water to be healed,' he told him. He held out his hand to Adam.

'Get up now, take up your mat and walk . . .'

As Adam stared blankly at the stranger, he suddenly felt a

tingling in his legs – legs that had been numb for years! Before he knew what he was doing, he had clasped the outstretched hand, and the next minute he was on his feet – standing!

Adam thought he must be dreaming! He stared down at his legs which had been useless only moments before. He bent his knees and wriggled his toes. It was unbelievable – and yet it was really true! For the first time in his life he was looking at the pool from a standing position!

'I can walk . . .' he whispered and turned to the stranger beside him. But the stranger had gone! While Adam had been examining his legs, he had slipped away into the crowd.

Adam stood for a moment, uncertain what to do. His heart was bursting with excitement and yet he was puzzled that the person responsible for this miracle had simply vanished. Who was this mystery man?

Craning his neck, Adam scanned the edges of the pool – but he could see no trace of him. What should he do now? Well, he would just have to do as the miracle-man had told him and take up his mat and walk!

Stooping down, he rolled up the mat he had been lying on for so many, many years. Several people nearby who had been watching him stared in amazement.

'Look, Adam's walking!' one exclaimed.

'I don't understand it,' another rejoindered. 'One minute he was lying there on his mat and the next he was standing up! Hey Adam . . .'

But Adam wasn't listening. Grinning from ear to ear he picked his way through the bodies stretched out on either side of the waters and headed away from the pool. It was a wonderful day and it was great to be alive!

'Hey, you – stop!' the voice behind him broke his reverie and Adam spun round to see a Pharisee hurrying up to him.

'What do you think you're doing?' the important looking little man puffed, his long beard bristling with indignation. He pointed at the mat under Adam's arm. 'Don't you know it's the Sabbath and it's against the law to carry your mat?'

Adam smiled. Here was someone he could share his good news with! Once the Pharisee knew all the wonderful facts, he would understand why he was breaking the law and rejoice with him!

'I'm carrying my mat because a man has just cured me!' he explained, his eyes shining with excitement. 'He told me to get up take up my mat and walk! You see, for thirty-eight years . . .'

'I beg your pardon!' interrupted the Pharisee, his face like thunder. What did you just say . . .?'

'A man healed me . . .' Adam faltered.

'You were cured on the Sabbath!' The Pharisee's face went red and his voice rose to a roar.' Who did this wicked thing?'

Adam stared at the ground, overcome with confusion. Didn't the Pharisee understand what had happened? Why didn't he want to share in his good news and joy? Was he so concerned about the mat that he didn't care that Adam's life had suddenly been changed?

'Well?' continued the enraged Pharisee. 'Who was it?'

'I . . . I don't know,' stammered Adam, his smile had disappeared and his head drooped.

'What do you mean you don't know?'

'Well, I was at the Pool of Bethzatha . . . and this stranger came up and said . . .' Adam stumbled over the words. 'Er . . . he told me to get off my mat and . . . and I did. When I looked up again he was gone . . .'

The Pharisee stared long and hard at Adam.

'Keep an eye out for this man,' he ordered finally. 'If you see him again, let me know.'

Adam nodded and hurried away, confused and unhappy. Perhaps someone who knew him would recognise him and be thrilled that he had been cured . . .'

Next day Adam was standing in the Temple when a man walked up to him. Adam recognised him immediately.

'You're the man who cured me yesterday by the pool!' he gasped.

'That's right,' the stranger smiled. 'I've come to tell you that you are well and your sins have been forgiven, but remember not to sin anymore.'

Adam nodded. 'I want to thank you for healing me,' he said. 'I was too surprised to say anything yesterday! But I don't even know who you are . . .'

'My name is Jesus,' replied the stranger.

Now Adam felt even more confused. He was so happy to be well again, and so grateful to the person who had made it possible – and yet . . . Adam was a good Jew, and he held the Pharisees in a great deal of awe. When one of them gave an order, Adam knew that it had to be obeyed . . .

Slowly, he walked out of the Temple, his brows knitted and his eyed fixed on the ground. He was so wrapped up in his thoughts that he hardly noticed when a group of Pharisees wandered by – until, that is, one of them pushed past him and almost knocked him over! As he hurriedly moved aside, Adam saw that it was the man who had shouted at him the day before.

'Excuse me!' he ventured, 'I'm sorry to disturb you sir, but the man I told you about – the one who cured me – he's here, in the Temple! He told me his name was Jesus . . .'

The Pharisees paused and glanced quickly at one another. One of them muttered something to his companions and then the group marched quickly past Adam, ignoring him in their anxiety not to miss Jesus.

Inside the Temple, Jesus stood and watched them approach. He had noticed how Adam had been pushed aside so abruptly and his brows were drawn in disapproval.

'Did you cure this man on the Sabbath?'

The first Pharisee made no effort to introduce himself or his companions. He stood in front of Jesus and questioned him loudly.

'That's right, I did,' Jesus replied, looking steadily into the questioner's eyes. 'He needed my help and I gave it.'

Another Pharisee butted in.

'But you know it's against the law to work on the Sabbath, don't you!' He shook his finger angrily at Jesus. 'You deliberately disobeyed it.'

'My Father, God, is always working,' Jesus replied. 'So I feel I should be working too.'

The Pharisees were speechless! They had expected Jesus to deny that he had broken the law – or at very least to look as if he was sorry! People were usually extra polite to the Pharisees, and careful how they answered them. And this Jesus had said that God was his own father – he had made himself equal to God! The Pharisees were so shocked they made no effort to stop Jesus as he turned from them and swept out of the Temple.

Once he had disappeared in the crowd, the angry group began to mutter furiously among themselves.

'He's dangerous!' The one who had pushed Adam decided. 'He's has no worries about breaking the law . . .'

'Not only that!' added his friend. 'He thinks that his father is God! The man's a blasphemer – or else a complete fool!'

The third Pharisee shook his head slowly. 'That man is no fool,' he decided. 'He's clever, and fearless – a danger to society. He must be dealt with!'

The little huddle all agreed.

Out in the sunshine, Adam was unaware of the confrontation which had just taken place. He stepped lightly down the narrow road which led from the Temple, enjoying the freedom which had been denied to him for so many years. Everything was wonderful – his life, which a few days before had seemed so dull and pointless, now stretched before him invitingly, and Adam was looking forward to the great adventure . . .

Not on the Sabbath

Anna shuffled towards the synagogue, leaning heavily on her walking stick. She moved very slowly, stopping after each step to steady herself, for the people who hurried past her on either side frequently bumped into her. They didn't do it deliberately – it was simply that they didn't see her until they were almost on top of her, for poor Anna was bent over double, looking at the ground. In fact, for years all she'd been able to see of the figures who passed her in the street were their sandals!

Eighteen years before, Anna had been very ill. The disease had affected her spine, leaving her back twisted so that she could no longer stand up properly. Now she relied on a stick for balance whenever she moved. Often she heard the voices of people as they passed her in the street – some were cruel and would laugh at her or make rude comments, but others felt sorry for her and tried to help as best they could. Anna couldn't look into people's faces – only little children were her height, and when Anna smiled at them they would often run away crying, alarmed by this peculiar, hunched-up little woman.

She had visited many doctors, but none of them had been able to help. Of course, they all claimed that they knew how to make her well again – but when it came to remedies, none of them worked! Her back was still twisted, and nobody seemed able to make it straight. Anna now accepted that she would be like this for the rest of her life. She tried to carry on as best she could, but she was so slow – much slower than anyone else.

Today was Saturday, the Sabbath, when the Jews went to the synagogue to worship. The short walk from her house was as laborious as ever – she'd lost count how many times people had bumped into her that morning! Some days Anna wondered if she'd ever get there. She sighed deeply to herself as she struggled along, pausing for a moment to let a group of people overtake her. As they hurried past, Anna caught a snippet of their conversation . . .

'Jesus is teaching in the synagogue today,' one man was telling his companions. ' I wonder what he'll have to say?'

'I saw him last week,' his friend replied. 'He healed a blind man in front of everyone – right there by the side of the road!'

'I've heard . . .' but the little group had swept past and she could no longer hear them.

Anna pondered on what she had heard as she continued her slow progress. She knew about this man Jesus – everyone did – but she'd never heard or seen him. Not that she could see him even if she was very close. She'd only be able to see as much of him as she could of everyone else – his feet! Even so, several times lately when Anna had heard that he was nearby she'd tried to go out to hear him. But she'd always missed him because she had been too slow. By the time she'd reached the spot where he'd been teaching, Jesus had moved away to another place.

She'd told her friends that she wanted to hear some of the wonderful stories he told, which was perfectly true – but Anna also had another, secret hope. If Jesus could make blind people see then maybe he could straighten her back! However, she had to be near him first. Perhaps today might be her lucky day!

As she entered the synagogue, Anna suddenly halted as she realised the hopelessness of her dream. How could she get close to Jesus when she didn't even know what he looked like? And she couldn't push her way through a crowd. Her dream of being cured had vanished again. There was no way she could possibly get near enough to Jesus for him to cure her.

Disappointed, Anna sighed sadly, wondering whether she should simply go home. However, now that she was here, she might as well listen to what he had to say! Her back might be crooked but that wouldn't stop her from listening to Jesus. Carefully she moved to one side of the synagogue out of the way of the people who were filing in and out. Leaning on her stick she listened to the man who was teaching from the Scriptures.

'Who is that speaking?' she asked someone close by.

'It's Jesus,' came the reply and Anna nodded. In her heart she had already known it was him – it had to be. Everything he said was so fresh and new. No wonder crowds of people followed him everywhere. She could stand there and listen to him for hours . . .

Abruptly the voice stopped and a murmur passed through the assembled audience. Anna was puzzled. She strained her head upwards to try and see what was going on – but it was no use, she just couldn't straighten up enough. She wondered why Jesus had stopped speaking – he couldn't have finished because he had paused in the middle of a sentence. Oh, why couldn't she lift her head up, just a little, to see what was happening?

Suddenly, a strange sensation passed through Anna. She shivered, feeling that every eye in the room was fixed on her, that she was for some reason the centre of attention. She managed to raise her face a tiny fraction, and realised that someone was standing in front of her.

As usual all she could see of the figure was the hem of his robe and two feet in sandals – so she had no idea who it was! Only when the person spoke did she realise it was the voice of the man who had been teaching the Scriptures – Jesus! He'd been speaking when he had suddenly noticed Anna's bent figure in the corner. He had felt so sorry for her that he interrupted his teaching and walked straight towards her. The people in the synagogue whispered amongst themselves about what might happen. They knew that something extraordinary usually happened when Jesus was around.

'You poor woman,' Jesus said tenderly to her. 'How long have you been like this?'

Although she couldn't see his face, Anna heard the kindness and pity in his voice. Immediately she forgot about the people watching and listening. It was as if Jesus and herself were the only people present.

'Eighteen years – and no one can tell me what's wrong . . .' she said, still looking at his feet. '. . . I've seen so many doctors and tried so many certain cures, but none of them have made any difference to me. All I know is that I'm doubled over like this, and unable to hold my head up high and walk tall.'

'Eighteen years!' he cried. 'And no one can help you?'

'I've hoped and prayed for a cure all this time but I'm still crippled – no one can help me!' she whispered.

'I'll help you,' he said. 'Woman, you are cured of your illness. Stand up straight!'

Amid gasps all about her, Anna felt Jesus' hand touch her back. She immediately felt a tingling feeling running up and down her spine, and a surge of power filling her body. Before she knew it she was standing upright! For the first time in eighteen years she wasn't bent over double. She was able to stand and walk properly, and see people's faces instead of their feet. It was wonderful. She was cured!

Anna stared at the man in front of her. She could now see the face belonging to the voice she had been listening to only seconds before. His was one of the few adult faces she had seen in eighteen years and it was one she would remember for the rest of her life – a face full of joy, understanding and kindness. How could she ever thank him enough for what he'd done for her?

'Oh thank you,' she whispered. 'Thank you!' She couldn't think of anything else to say.

'Go home and be happy,' he said smiling at her.

Grinning widely Anna looked about her. She gazed at the decoration of the synagogue, the sunlight streaming through the windows and doors. She saw faces. They were all different and she stared at every single one. Everything was so wonderful and so new she tried to look in all directions at once, swivelling her head about so as not to miss anything or anyone. There were smiling faces everywhere! Some were friends whose voices she recognised and others were strangers, but all were eager to join in her happiness . . .

. . . but not everyone. At that moment with the excitement growing by the second, a leader of the synagogue spoke loudly from the opposite side of the building.

'This is disgusting!' he boomed. 'There are six days in the week for people to be healed. We all know that healing is working and everyone also knows that no one is allowed to work on the Sabbath.' He glared across at Anna. 'So if you wanted to be healed you should have come another day, but not today. Not on the Sabbath.'

The excitement in the synagogue died instantly and the smile disappeared from Anna's face as she stared first at the official and then at Jesus. What was he talking about? Wasn't he pleased that she was no longer in pain?

Then another thought flashed through her head. Perhaps Jesus, realising his mistake, would somehow make her ill again and tell her to come back tomorrow to be healed. Oh no, she couldn't bear that! Surely he wouldn't do that!

There was a hushed silence as everyone waited.

'Don't be so silly,' he cried angrily to the official. 'Are laws more important than people?'

He paused, but as the man didn't answer, he continued, 'You say I am breaking the law, but even your own rules allow you to untie an animal or give it a drink on the Sabbath, don't they?'

Still the official said nothing, but several people murmured. 'Yes, that's true.'

'And isn't that working?' asked Jesus.

'Yes – yes!' came the replies, louder this time as more people joined in.

'So if you can help an animal on the Sabbath, why can't I help this poor woman, a descendant of Abraham and Sarah who has suffered so long? I could have cured her tomorrow, but why wait? Why should she suffer one minute longer than she has to?'

The official shuffled his feet as he looked down at the floor. He glanced sideways at his friends but they looked the other way. Jesus had made the Pharisees look petty and small minded.

'He's right!' the crowd agreed. 'People are more important than laws.'

Secretly they were pleased that the synagogue official had been so embarrassed. They clustered around Anna chattering excitedly about the events they had just witnessed.

Anna hardly heard them. She was too busy thanking God for the wonderful thing that had happened.

Everyone who had seen the miracle had learned an important lesson. We must help others whenever they need us and not just when the laws say we should!

Anna turned to catch a last glimpse of the man who had healed her and lifted up her hand to wave her thanks. Jesus saw her and smiled and waved in return. He was then lost among the crowd of people as they surged out of the building to tell others what they'd seen and heard that day.

'I've found it!'

'Joanna, I'm going to the well now. Are you ready?'

A woman in a long, softly flowing, sky blue gown stood outside a house in a stony street. Her hair was covered with a close fitting cap, decorated with silver coins, and over it she wore a long, white veil which she had pulled across her mouth. On her head she carried a large water-pot, balanced comfortably on a padded ring. She tapped her foot as she heard her friend moving about inside her home.

'All right, Hannah, I'm coming now.' Joanna hurried outside carrying her jug in one hand. She was dressed in a bright yellow gown and wore gold coins sewn to her head dress. Carefully balancing the empty jug on her padded ring, she joined her friend and the two women hurried off towards their village well.

The well was quite a long walk away. As it was now late afternoon, it was much cooler than it had been earlier in the day, and the two women met up with many others who were also making the evening journey – the only water available for use in their homes was what they carried home in their jugs. Some of the women had to make several trips to the well every day to get enough water! Hannah and Joanna chatted together as they waited in line, listening to all the latest gossip. The well was always the best place to catch up on any news in the village!

Their turn came, and they filled their jugs to the brim with the cool water, carefully balancing them on their heads ready for the slow walk home. The jugs were very heavy – but the women were so used to carrying them that they hardly spilt a drop of the precious liquid. As they walked, they continued to discuss the news they had heard at the well, and talk about the people they'd seen.

'Poor Martha didn't look very well today,' confided Joanna. 'She shouldn't have to carry water when she's so ill. And she has so far to walk . . .'

'I know,' Hannah agreed, 'but who else is there to carry water for her? Her sons are strong and healthy but they won't do it. They say it's women's work. Huh! I'm sure they wouldn't like to carry a heavy jug of water on their heads as far as their mother does!'

The two friends paused for a moment as they remembered the frail, bent old lady who had struggled with her jug of water to and from the well. They would have liked to help her but there wasn't time to carry her water and do all their own jobs at home as well. It took so long to walk anywhere carrying a heavy water-pot!

'Miriam's new baby is looking very well,' Hannah remarked, changing the subject. 'Mind you, I still don't think she swaddles him firmly enough. I always made sure that my children were bound up really tightly – and look how strong and sturdy the twins turned out!'

Her friend nodded. Hannah was something of an expert when it came to advice on child rearing. 'Plenty of olive-oil rubs – that's the secret,' she continued, as Joanna's house came into sight. 'Olive-oil rubs and a good dusting of powdered myrtle at every change! Well, here we are home again . . . by the way, Joanna, I meant to ask you earlier – what have you done to your head-dress? One of the gold coins is missing . . .'

Joanna stopped so suddenly that some of the water slopped over the rim of her pot.

'What do you mean?' she exclaimed.

'. . . the third from the left isn't there . . .'

'It must be!' Joanna's face whitened. 'That's not funny, Hannah!'

'I'm not joking,' replied Hannah, looking a little put out. 'That coin is definitely not there. Didn't you know?'

The two friends put their jugs down and Joanna hastily put both hands up to feel her head dress. Both women wore little caps beneath their veils, gaily decorated with coins. Usually, Joanna had ten golden coins jingling against her forehead, but now, as she felt them with her fingers, she could only count nine! Again and again she frantically counted – but each time she only reached nine. There was an empty space where one of the coins should hang. Hannah was right – one of her precious coins was missing!

'When did you notice it was gone?' she asked distractedly. It could have fallen off anywhere, she thought – on the way to fetch the water, on the road back, somewhere in the house

. . . tears filled Joanna's eyes as she imagined the precious gold coin lying under the water at the bottom of the well!

Her head dress was the most precious thing she owned. It represented the entire family savings – her whole dowry – and now one of the coins was missing. She'd never be able to replace it!

She was so deep in thought that she didn't hear Hannah's answer.

'I . . . I'm sorry, what did you say?' she mumbled. 'When did you say you saw it was missing?'

'I said that I saw it was gone as soon as you came out of the house to go to the well,' Hannah repeated.

'Why didn't you say something then?' cried Joanna.

'I was going to – but then I started talking and it slipped my mind. You know what I'm like when I've got some interesting news . . . I'm sorry, Joanna – I should have said something earlier.'

Hannah looked upset.

'It's all right,' Joanna reassured her friend. 'It isn't your fault. I'm just upset. You are sure it was missing when I left the house?'

'Yes,' nodded Hannah. 'Quite sure.'

'Oh,' Joanna breathed. 'Well, that's a relief anyway! At least I don't have to walk back along that long stony road searching for it. Can you imagine finding a coin along there? I was also worried that it might have fallen into the well . . .'

'What a horrible thought!' shuddered Hannah, fingering her own head dress to make sure all her coins were in place. 'But we must think where it can be . . .'

'It must be in the house somewhere,' decided Joanna. She frowned. 'Or then again it could be outside . . . But I haven't been outside today except to go to the well, so the best idea would be to start looking inside first . . .'

'Would you like me to help you?' asked her friend. She knew how much the coins of the head dress meant to Joanna.

'No – no, Hannah,' Joanna replied shaking her head. 'Thanks for asking, but I know you've your own work to do. I'll search by myself. You never know, it may be just inside the door . . .'

'Perhaps,' agreed Hannah, trying to look hopeful. 'Oh well, I'll come back when my work's finished to see how you're getting on.'

While Hannah replaced her water jug on her head and set off down the road to her home, Joanna was already searching the ground outside her front door. After a while she shook her head sadly, picked up her jug, and carried it inside to the cool kitchen.

With the sun sinking in the western sky her house was quite dark. The one small window in the room didn't allow much light to enter the house even during the day. As she peered about her, her spirits fell, for no glint of a shiny coin caught her eye. However would she find such a small coin? Where should she start?

Heaving a deep sigh, she lit her small lamp and placed it on the table. It spread a circle of light in the centre of the room, but the rest of the house was still very dim. Joanna fetched her broom and began sweeping slowly and carefully. Then she got down on her hands and knees to move the rushes which were strewn on the floor, one by one, handful by handful. Carefully she sifted through them, hoping every second to see a tell-tale sparkle or hear a tinkle of her coin.

For nearly an hour she searched, sometimes sweeping and at other times down on her hands and knees, feeling over the floor using her fingers like a comb. All the time frantic thoughts raced through her head – what had she done that day, where had she worked, did she remember hearing the coin fall at any time? Although the evening was cool, Joanna was by now very hot. Perspiration covered her face as she searched and searched and she panicked inside at the thought that she may never find her coin again.

Suddenly she heard a knock at the door and a voice crying out,

'Aunty Joanna, are you in there?'

Joanna looked up from her kneeling position as her niece, Sarah, entered. Sarah stared with surprise at her aunt on her hands and knees in the middle of the floor. Joanna, who was a particularly neat and tidy person, now looked terrible! Stray pieces of hair were falling over her face and her beautiful yellow gown was filthy. It looked as if she'd been crawling around the floor in it.

'What are you doing, Aunty?' Sarah asked. 'Are you saying your prayers?'

'No, I'm not!' replied Joanna sharply, trying to brush back a piece of hair. She turned round to look at the little girl and smiled as she saw the worried expression on her face.

'I'm sorry, Sarah dear – I didn't mean to snap at you! But I've lost one of the coins from my head dress and I've been looking everywhere for it.' Her face fell again. 'It's no use though – I just can't find it . . .'

'Oh Aunty!' Sarah exclaimed. 'Where did you drop it?'

Her aunt rose to her feet, placing her hands on her hips.

'If I knew where I'd dropped it I wouldn't be down on my hands and knees looking for it, would I?'

'No,' grinned Sarah. 'I suppose you wouldn't! But I meant did you lose it in here or outside? Maybe I could help . . .'

'I think I lost it in here,' sighed Joanna, 'but I've been over the floor again and again and I still can't find it! I don't think I could have dropped it outside, but perhaps I did after all . . . If you'd like to look outside that would be a help. I really don't know where it could be.'

Her aunt knelt down again to continue searching but Sarah remained in the doorway, watching her.

'When I'm married I shall have a head dress like yours,' she informed Joanna. 'It's quite the nicest one that I've seen! Gold coins are prettier than silver, I think – but they do cost a lot of money, don't they, Aunty?'

'That's right,' answered Joanna, without looking round. 'And that's why it's so important that I find this coin. I'll never be able to buy another one!'

Sarah then turned and began to search outside, sifting through the dust and turning over the stones near the front door. She hoped she would find it because Aunt Joanna was her favourite aunt and she didn't like to see her so unhappy.

Back in the house Joanna had almost given up hope. Tears pricked at her eyes as thoughts chased through her head. Perhaps Hannah had been mistaken. Maybe she had lost it on the way to fetch the water after all. Worse still – maybe her precious coin was now lying at the bottom of the deep well, where she would never see it again! What was the use of looking any more? Oh, why did this have to happen to her?

Tears blurred her eyes and she quickly brushed them away with the back of her hand. It was hard enough trying to see in this dim light, crying would only make things worse.

Just then she saw a tiny glint in the far corner. She had searched in that corner about three times before and had seen nothing, but now she sat up straight and stared. Perhaps it had been her tears that had caught the light, or perhaps she had simply imagined it. Swiftly she crawled over to the corner, not daring to take her eyes from the spot, and then carefully and very gently moved the rushes that covered the floor. Suddenly a tell-tale tinkle was heard and in the next

second Joanna was holding her coin in shaking fingers. She had found it! She'd no idea how it had rolled into that corner – she couldn't even remember being near that part of the room that day. But it didn't matter now. Nothing mattered except for the fact that she had found her precious lost coin.

'Sarah, Sarah, come quickly!' she called, jumping to her feet. 'I've found it! I've found it!'

Sarah rushed inside to find her aunt dancing around the room, holding the gold coin in her hand, waving it above her head. Joanna grabbed her by the hands and they danced and laughed together.

'Isn't it wonderful?' laughed Joanna. 'I was so afraid I had lost it forever, but now, look . . . I've found it.'

'I'm so glad for you Aunty,' cried Sarah, gasping for breath. 'You looked so upset when I came in.'

'I was upset, but all that's forgotten now. I must go and tell Hannah. In fact I'll tell the whole street – the whole town. Everyone must know my wonderful news!'

Together they ran out into the street holding hands and laughing. Hannah, who had at that moment been hurrying up the street paused when she saw them. The worried look disappeared from her face as she saw Joanna and Sarah skipping and laughing. They wouldn't be doing that if the coin was still lost.

'Hannah,' Joanna cried, 'I've found it! I've found it!' she held the coin up for her friend to see. 'It was in a corner where I couldn't see it, but I searched and searched. It took a long time but here it is.'

Women ran from their houses to discover what all the shouting was all about. It wasn't long before Joanna's story had been told and retold, and soon all the women had forgotten their household jobs and were laughing and dancing, singing and crying together, joining in Joanna's happiness. They all knew how precious the coins were and how they would have felt if they had lost one of the coins from their own head dresses.

They joined in a circle and cheered as Joanna fixed the coin firmly back in place. She beamed around at them all, knowing that they shared in her joy in finding the lost coin. What a story she would be able to tell the other women tomorrow at the well!

The generous gift

Jesus and his disciples were sitting in the cool courtyard outside the Temple. Every day the men and women of Jerusalem came and placed their gifts of money into the offering boxes that were kept there. This money helped to pay for the Temple expenses.

The courtyard was also a place where people often met one another. They would stand and discuss the latest news or just sit and watch the almost constant stream of people enter, drop their money into a box and leave.

Jesus and his friends had just come from the Temple and had sat down a little way from the boxes to relax. It was busy in the courtyard today. The air buzzed with the sounds of people walking, talking and money tinkling.

Some of the disciples talked quietly amongst themselves while others leaned back lazily, watching the people go in and out. One or two of them thought it was an excellent chance to catch up on some sleep and closed their eyes.

Peter was taking a keen interest in the people entering and leaving the courtyard. He nudged John who sat beside him.

'It's busy in here today, isn't it?' he said.

John had his eyes closed and was almost asleep. He opened one eye, glanced around the courtyard quickly and then closed it again.

'Um,' he answered, giving a very slight nod of his head. His arms were folded across his chest and his head drooped down a little onto them. He wasn't interested.

'Look at all the money going into those boxes,' said Peter, again nudging him.

John didn't even bother to open his eyes this time but grunted, wishing Peter would leave him alone. He was tired.

But Peter felt like talking to someone. He turned to talk to Jesus who was sitting next to him on the other side, but Jesus was talking with Andrew. Turning back to John he tried again.

'Don't you think it's interesting watching people?'

'No,' answered John grumpily, his eyes still firmly shut. He wriggled about slightly, trying to find a more comfortable position.

'Oh I do,' Peter continued cheerfully. 'Every single person is so different. You can tell so much about a person by the way they dress or even walk. Don't you think so?'

There was no reply.

'Now take that man for instance.'

John's eyes suddenly opened as Peter dug him sharply in the ribs. He sat up alert and groaned, knowing any chance of sleep had gone. Why had he sat next to Peter? He rubbed his side tenderly, his eyes following Peter's finger.

The man whom Peter had found so interesting was easy to spot in the crowd of people milling about in the courtyard. He was tall with a smug look on his face. As he walked slowly to the offering boxes people moved back out of his way. His

robe was a rich deep blue made from a very expensive, soft material. Everyone realised he was a rich and powerful man.

John watched with growing interest as he strolled up to an offering box. Very carefully he took a bag of money from under his long flowing robe. Slowly he untied it and dropped the glittering coins from the bag into the box.

'That's a lot of money,' whispered John.

Peter agreed, pleased that he had at last caught John's attention.

'He made sure everyone knew he was giving so much, though,' said Peter grimly. 'Those coins made such a noise.'

The man had now re-tied his bag, a jewelled ring flashing on his finger. He replaced the bag under his robes and turned to leave. Many people stopped to stare at his tall figure as he glided out of the Treasury.

'The Temple officials would be pleased if everyone gave as much as that,' said John. He had now forgotten about being tired and was as interested as Peter in what was happening in the courtyard.

They watched in silence as more people entered and placed their money in the boxes. A woman caught John's attention and he nudged Peter.

'See that woman over there . . . just coming in,' he said pointing. 'I'm sure she'll give a large donation.'

They watched as the woman, elegantly dressed in a red and white robe approached a box. Her expensive jewellery glittered and jangled as she opened the bag she was carrying.

'Do you know her?' asked Peter.

'Oh no, I don't know anyone who has that much money,' laughed John. 'But I've heard about her from friends and I've seen her in here before.'

While they watched, the woman's offering trickled into the offering box – a stream of silver coins. When the bag was empty, she folded it and tucked it out of sight in the folds of her robe. Peter and John gazed after her as she left the courtyard.

'What do you know about her?' asked Peter curiously.

'She lives in an enormous white house a few streets away,' said John. 'I'll show you later if you like. She is very rich and has many servants.'

Peter nodded his head. 'I think I know the house you mean. You were certainly right about her offering. I've never seen so much money! She was very generous to give so much to the Temple.'

Again they sat in silence as men and women, young and old, came and went. Then Peter's attention was drawn to another woman who had entered the Treasury. Perhaps he noticed her because she was so different from the lady they had been discussing before.

'I don't think this woman's offering will help the Temple much,' he said.

John too saw her enter. She was a small woman, slightly bent who shuffled towards the offering boxes. Her clothes were ragged and grubby, her face sad and wrinkled. She was old, slow and poor. They watched as she stopped at a box but no one else in the courtyard took any notice of her. No one turned to watch or move out of her way as they had done to the rich man and woman who had come in earlier. Her clothes weren't of a fine material and she wore no jewellery at all. And her offering? Peter and John could see that she held something very tiny in her hand.

'She has one coin to offer,' said John. 'No, no, it's two coins.'

'One coin or two, it doesn't make any difference,' said Peter sighing. 'Those coins are nearly worthless anyway. It's hardly worthwhile giving those coins to the Temple. They won't help.'

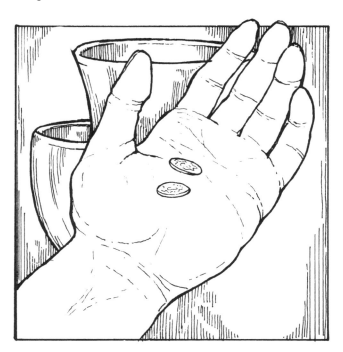

'No. It's not like those large bags of money we saw earlier,' agreed John. 'Those people were very generous with their money and gave much more.'

'That's where you're wrong.'

Peter and John jumped. They had been concentrating so hard on the old woman they hadn't noticed that Jesus had stopped talking with Andrew and had been listening to them.

'We were just saying . . .' Peter began.

'I know what you've been saying,' interrupted Jesus. 'I've been listening to you for quite a while.'

'Why did you say we were wrong?' asked John.

'You're wrong about how generous that poor woman is with her money,' said Jesus.

'Wrong?' asked Peter. 'But you didn't see earlier . . .'

'The rich woman – the one from the large house with all the servants? The one who gave a bag of silver coins?' asked Jesus.

'Yes,' said John. 'And the man before her – the one in the blue robe with the large ring on his finger. He gave a large donation too.'

'I know,' said Jesus quietly. 'I saw them.'

Peter was amazed. All the time Jesus had been talking to Andrew he had been watching the people as well. He wondered how much of his conversation with John, Jesus had overheard.

'They gave a lot of money,' Jesus continued. 'But that doesn't mean that they were generous.'

Peter and John looked at each other. Whatever did Jesus mean?

'I don't understand,' said Peter, puzzled.

Jesus moved his eyes in the woman's direction and they all watched her place the coins into the box. The coins were so small they didn't make any noise as they fell. She then turned slowly and shuffled outside into the sunshine, unaware that she was the topic of a conversation.

Jesus turned back to Peter. 'Do you know anything about that woman?' he asked.

Peter and John both shrugged their shoulders and shook their heads.

'She was just a poor woman,' said Peter.

'That's true,' said Jesus. 'Poor and also a widow. Her husband had been ill for a long time before he died and what little money they did have was spent on doctors. They didn't have much money before he died but now she has very little.'

'That's why she could only give those two small coins,' said Peter.

'Yes, because that's all she had,' said Jesus. 'And that's why her gift has been the most generous of all that have been offered today.'

The two disciples stared at Jesus amazed. Did he really mean that the widow's offering of two tiny worthless coins was greater than the bags of silver coins which had been offered? It didn't make sense.

Jesus saw that they were still puzzled.

'You still don't understand, do you?' he said. 'You are still looking at the size of the offering. A bag of silver coins seems to be worth much more than two tiny coins, doesn't it?'

Peter and John agreed. That was right.

'But the size of the gift is not important,' Jesus explained. 'The rich man and woman could afford to give a bag of money. They won't even miss it because they have many more bags of coins at home.'

'But the widow . . .?' Peter asked.

'But the widow gave all the money she had,' Jesus replied. 'Her two coins were all she had to live on and she gave them both away. Now she has nothing left.'

Peter and John sat deep in thought. Now they understood what Jesus had been saying and they wondered what the widow would do.

'I suppose she could have given only one coin to the Temple and kept the other for herself,' said John slowly. 'It wouldn't have been much but it would have been something.'

'But she didn't,' said Jesus. 'She gave everything she had, and because of that her offering is the most generous one of all.'

'I can see!'

Philip sat in his usual place near the gate of the Temple. For as long as he could remember he had come here every day to beg for coins from those who passed. He had been blind ever since he was born and begging was the only way he could earn a living.

Many people passed him today because it was the Sabbath and they were on their way to the Temple. He sighed and shifted slightly into a more comfortable position. The ground was hard and he had been sitting there for quite a while.

Even though he was blind, Philip knew what was happening about him. He could hear the sound of footsteps approaching and then quicken as they hurried past. Sometimes friends would stop and chat with him about the latest news or weather. He heard, too, the comments of people as they walked by him.

'There's another beggar hoping for money.'

'Is he lame?'

'No, I think that one's blind.'

'Good, he can't see us. Let's hurry on.'

Philip was used to conversations like this. However, today he suddenly pricked up his ears. Some men were talking about him and asking a question he had often asked himself. He strained hard to hear what was being said.

'Teacher,' a voice said, 'see that beggar there beside the gate.'

There was no answer, so the voice continued.

'I've been told that he's been blind since he was born. Whose fault was that – his or his parents?'

Philip was very interested in the answer and leaned closer to the voices, hoping they didn't notice him listening.

There was a slight pause before another voice answered,

'It isn't anyone's fault this man is blind,' he said. 'He isn't being punished because he or his parents did something wrong. The only important thing about this blind man is what God's power can do in his life.'

The questioner mumbled something which Philip didn't hear. He was thinking hard. What did this man mean and who was he? How he wished he could see what was happening right in front of him! He felt so helpless.

'I want to help you.'

The words suddenly broke through Philip's thoughts and made him jump slightly. The speaker was right in front of him.

'Who are you . . .?' Philip cried, a little frightened. 'And what can you do for me?'

'My name is Jesus,' came the quiet reply, 'and if you'll let me, I'll help you to see.'

Philip trembled from head to foot. Here was a perfect stranger; someone he'd never met before, saying that he could do what Philip had dreamed of, ever since he was a little boy. To be able to see was all he had ever wanted and here suddenly was a man who was saying he could help him.

'I . . . I don't understand,' he stammered and then stopped. He must be dreaming.

'Don't worry about anything,' said Jesus. 'I'll tell you exactly what I'm going to do. I'm going to make some mud by spitting on the dust on the road.'

Philip waited as Jesus knelt on the dusty ground and mixed some dust with his saliva to make a muddy pasty ointment.

Then Jesus continued. 'Now I'm going to put the mud I've made on your eyes.'

If Philip was surprised, so were Jesus' friends who had been watching carefully.

'What's he doing?' asked one. 'I've never seen Jesus do this before.'

The others shrugged their shoulders, waited and watched. Philip sat still while Jesus rubbed on the muddy ointment.

'Now,' said Jesus, standing up and helping Philip to his feet, 'I've done my part. It's now your turn to do something. I want you to go to the Pool of Siloam and wash the mud off your face.'

'Is that all I have to do?' asked Philip. 'Just go and wash my face?'

'That's right,' Jesus replied.

'All right, I'll go straight away,' said Philip and immediately set off with his stick, feeling his way to the Pool.

He grinned as he realised what a funny sight he must be with the mud, drying quickly in the sunshine, covering his eyes. But he didn't care. This was the first time in his whole life that someone had given him hope that he could see, and he was going to do exactly as he was told, no matter how silly he appeared to others.

Suddenly a little doubt crept into his mind. Perhaps this was all a joke. Those men could have used him for a nasty practical joke and were even now laughing together at the sight of a foolish blind man walking along the road with mud covering his face.

'No,' thought Philip firmly. 'That's not true. He seemed so sincere. I know that he wanted to help.'

He then remembered snippets of conversations he'd overheard of people who had been healed recently by a man – women who were lame, men who were dumb . . .

'I wonder,' he said aloud. 'Could this be the same man?'

'What did you say?' A woman's voice startled him.

'Oh nothing,' Philip mumbled. 'I was only thinking aloud.'

'Do you know you have mud caked all over your face?' she asked, concerned. 'Let me help you clean it off . . .'

'Oh no,' cried Philip hastily. 'I'm going to the Pool of Siloam to wash the mud off my face. It's very important that I go there.'

'All right.' The woman sounded unsure. 'The pool is just over to your right; you're nearly there.'

'Thank you,' said Philip, and still guided by his stick, changed direction. He could smell the water and minutes later his feet were splashing through it.

He hesitated a moment, took a deep breath, whispered to himself. 'Well, here we go!' and splashed the water onto his face. Again and again he scooped the water up onto his eyes and rubbed. He could feel the mud sliding down his face into the pool and then almost without thinking Philip opened his eyes and he could see!

He blinked several times at the brilliant sunshine, but nothing could tempt him to close his eyes again. For the first time in his life he could see trees, the water in the pool, the greens and browns of the surrounding countryside. It was wonderful! It was a miracle!

He jumped up and down and splashed in the water, shouting at the top of his voice, 'I can see! I can see!'

He threw his stick away and ran and danced and skipped down the road he had just so painfully crept along as a blind man.

Racing past a woman like a whirlwind, he shouted back at her, 'I'm cured – I'm cured! It worked!'

She stared at his rapidly disappearing figure and shook her head, bewildered.

'That's the second strange man I've met today,' she thought. 'I'd better hurry home in case there are any more about!'

It wasn't long before Philip slowed down so that he could look about him and see the beauty of nature he had missed out on for so long. As he neared the town, however, he slowed his footsteps even more. A thought suddenly entered his head. Would he be able to find his way home, now that he could see? For years he had relied on his instincts to find his way about, but now everything was different and unfamiliar.

But he didn't have to worry. As he wandered along the road, staring at houses that had surrounded him all his life – but only now seeing them for the first time – Philip stumbled on some rough stones. Immediately he knew these stones were outside his own house. How many times had he stubbed a foot on them in the past!

He stared open-mouthed at his home for a full minute

before running in through the door, eager to share his good news with his family.

'Mum! Dad!' he shouted, bursting through the doorway. 'I can see! I can see! I met a man called Jesus and he put mud on my eyes and I washed it off in the Pool of Siloam and now I can see.'

As the words tumbled out, his parents and the rest of his family rushed in from all directions to find out what all the shouting was about.

Suddenly there was a startled silence. The voices Philip had heard all his life now had faces, but they were so different from what he had imagined them to be. And what a shock for his family! The blind son and brother who had left the house as usual a few hours before had now come home able to see! And what a story! Even though he repeated it over and over again, it still sounded impossible.

It was a long time before the family realised what had happened, but even then they couldn't understand it.

The news of Philip's sight spread quickly amongst his friends and neighbours, and by the next day a great crowd was milling around outside his home. Arguments broke out as the people talked amongst themselves about what had happened.

'Isn't it wonderful?' said one woman, excitedly. 'Philip has been cured of his blindness after all these years.'

'I tell you it's not Philip,' growled a deep voice beside her. 'Philip sits outside the Temple and begs. I see him everyday. This man just looks like him.'

'Don't be silly!' cried another voice. 'Of course it's Philip.'

'No,' said another. 'Someone born blind can't just suddenly see.'

'It's not true,' shouted someone else.

At that moment, Philip, hearing the noise, came out of the house.

'Here he is. Ask him yourself!' called a voice from the crowd. 'Go on – ask him!'

Everyone turned to Philip who held up his hands for silence.

'I know some of you find it hard to understand,' he said, 'but what you have heard is true. I am the man who used to sit by the gate of the Temple and beg because I was blind – but I have now been cured!'

'How?' The question came from all parts of the crowd.

'My story is strange but simple,' Philip explained. 'A man

called Jesus put mud on my eyes and told me to wash it off in the Pool of Siloam. I did this and immediately I could see.'

As Philip finished, the people muttered amongst themselves. They had never heard such a tale.

'Where is this Jesus now?' a woman asked.

'Yes, where is he?' chorused several others.

'I don't know.' Philip shrugged his shoulders. 'I don't even know what he looks like.'

Again the people whispered amongst themselves and there was a general nodding of heads. A man stepped forward and spoke clearly. 'We think your story is so important you should come and tell the Pharisees.'

Philip glanced behind him at his parents, then at the crowd. He nodded.

'All right, I'll come with you,' he said, and immediately set off, followed by his parents and a procession of curious onlookers.

An hour later he stood in front of the court of the Pharisees. They were all dressed in white and were seated on a raised platform, looking very stern and bored.

The Pharisees had heard a little of the story from a member of the crowd – but really! The story was so fanciful. Were they really expected to believe such a tale?

'Tell us how you were cured,' said a priest in a most disinterested manner. Oh dear! There was a mark on his robe. That must be attended to as soon as possible!'

Philip stood up as straight as he could and repeated his story yet again.

'A man called Jesus rubbed mud on my eyes and told me to wash it off in the Pool of Siloam.'

'And when did this happen?' asked another bored voice.

'On the Sabbath,' Philip replied. 'I was sitting . . .'

'On the Sabbath!' The Pharisees leant forward as one. Now they were interested! It was the law that no work – including healing – was to be done on the Sabbath. Who had dared to break this rule?

'Who was this man, did you say?' a Pharisee asked, glaring at Philip.

'I . . . I don't know anything about him,' Philip replied, 'but I believe he must be a prophet.'

'You say you were blind from birth?' another asked him.

'Yes,' Philip answered.

The Pharisees leaned close to one another and muttered

amongst themselves. When they were seated again, one spoke.

'We've listened to your story and quite frankly we don't believe it,' he said. 'We want to check with your parents that you really were blind at birth.'

Whispering broke out amongst the onlookers as a guard called Philip's parents. They stood next to their son in front of the court, looking frightened. A tall pharisee leant forward.

'We want to know,' he growled, 'if this is your son.'

'He certainly is!' Philip's father replied.

'You also say he was born blind, and yet he can now see!' continued the questioner. 'How did this happen?'

Philip's mother stared at the priest. She knew the Pharisees were very powerful and gave her answer nervously, her voice trembling.

'It is true that my son was born blind,' she told him. 'It is also true that he can now see. But we don't know how this has happened or who cured him.'

'Perhaps you should ask him yourself,' Philip's father added more boldly. 'He's old enough to speak for himself.'

The Pharisee stared long and hard at the two parents before moving his attention back to Philip.

'Well,' he said. 'Tell me. Who cured you and how did he do it?'

By this time, Philip's patience had run out. He didn't care any more that he was before a Pharisee court. He had had enough!

'What are you talking about?' he exploded angrily. 'I've told you, and I've told these people over and over again!' He spun around and pointed to the watching crowd. 'Haven't you been listening to anything I've said? I'm not going to repeat myself anymore!'

The Pharisees glowered at him. They hadn't expected this!

'You're a troublemaker,' one said. 'I think you're a follower of that man you say cured you on the Sabbath, and he's probably a troublemaker too.'

'You might think he's a troublemaker, but I think he's a man from God,' said Philip suddenly. 'How could he perform such a miracle otherwise?'

A startled gasp came from the Pharisees and onlookers alike and it took a moment or two for the Pharisees to recover. The leader then stood up, his face purple with rage.

'How dare you tell us who comes from God!' he roared. 'You have no training or right to do so. We don't believe you were cured – in fact, we don't believe you were blind in the first place! As a punishment for what you just said, you will not be allowed to enter the synagogue any more for the rest of your life!'

Philip stared in dismay at the Pharisees as they rose stiffly from their chairs and left the room. Realising it was all over, the crowd of onlookers also filed out, glancing cautiously over their shoulders at Philip. When they had all gone, Philip and his parents followed in silence.

Philip's mind was in a whirl. Why couldn't the Pharisees be happy for him instead of punishing him in this way? He was still happy at being able to see, but they had spoilt it for him. However, no matter what anyone said, he still felt that what he had said was right.

The next day Philip wandered alone through the streets, marvelling at all he could see. The news had spread that he had been thrown out of the synagogue, and everyone knew that this meant they weren't allowed to talk to him. He had offended the Pharisees and he was to be punished. So he was very surprised when a man stopped him in the street and addressed him.

'I heard you were expelled from the synagogue,' said the stranger, 'I've been searching for you all day.'

Philip stared at the man. He knew he had never seen him before and yet his voice was familiar. He had recognised people all his life by their voices, but for the moment he couldn't place this one. He knew he had heard it – but where and when?

'Do you believe in the Son of God?' the stranger asked abruptly.

This brought Philip up with a jolt! Who was this man who broke all the rules by speaking to him and asking such a question?

'I would believe in him if I knew who he was,' he replied boldly.

The stranger smiled. 'You've already met him,' he told Philip. 'In fact – you're talking to him now!'

Suddenly Philip understood! He knew why this man's voice had seemed so familiar. He had never seen the face before, but he knew where he had heard the voice. This man was Jesus – the one who had healed him. Was he the Son of

God? Of course! Who else would have the power to heal a man born blind?

'I told the Pharisees that you were a man from God,' Philip whispered. 'But I never thought you were the Son of God.'

'Do you believe in me?' asked Jesus.

'I believe in you, Lord,' Philip cried, tears welling in his eyes as he knelt before Jesus. 'Thank you for giving me my sight! And I do believe that you are the Son of God!'

Jesus helped the man to his feet. 'Go and be happy in your life,' he smiled. 'Not only are you able to see with your eyes, but you can also see with your heart! Many people born with perfect sight do not see as much as you!'

Philip watched Jesus go, and then continued on his way along the deserted street. There was a wide smile on his face and his eyes were shining.

'If only you'd been here . . .'

Mary and Martha were worried because their brother Lazarus had been ill for several weeks and wasn't improving.

'I don't know what we can do!' cried Martha. 'I've given him the medicine from the doctor but it hasn't made any difference to him at all.'

'He's becoming weaker every day.' Mary looked pale and exhausted, her voice trembling. 'He has such a high fever and he's in terrible pain.'

They sat together in the kitchen wondering what else they could do for their brother. Martha had made some soup that morning but Lazarus hadn't been able to eat any of it. They felt so helpless – and afraid that if he didn't improve soon, he could die!

'I think we should send a message to Jesus, letting him know how ill Lazarus is,' sniffed Mary after a few minutes' silence.

'That's a good idea,' agreed Martha. 'He'll come straight away if we ask him, I know.'

So the two sisters sent a messenger to find Jesus and tell him about his friend Lazarus.

It took the messenger several days to find Jesus, but when he finally did discover him in a distant town and gave him the news, Jesus just nodded and thanked him.

'Tell them I'll come,' he said, and the messenger returned to Mary and Martha. But Jesus didn't seem to be in a hurry to get to Bethany – in fact, it was two more days before he decided to leave. When he mentioned to his disciples that he was returning, they were surprised and alarmed.

'But Master!' cried John, 'It could be dangerous if you go back there!'

'That's right,' Thomas agreed. 'The last time we were in Jerusalem the people tried to kill us, and Bethany is only three kilometres from Jerusalem. Someone is sure to discover that we are there. They may try to kill us again!'

The disciples were all of one mind. They could remember, only too well, how nasty the people had turned in Jerusalem. The crowds hadn't liked what Jesus had been telling them and had started to throw stones at his disciples. The friends had only just escaped by running out of the city! If they had stayed a moment longer, they would surely have been killed. Some of them still had bruises all over where the stones had hit them! No, it would be foolish for them to return to that part of the country again so soon. There were plenty of other places Jesus could go where they'd all be safe.

However, Jesus had made up his mind.

'I must go to Bethany,' he said. 'Lazarus has died, and Martha and Mary need me . . .'

The disciples were even more surprised to hear this news. They hadn't known about it, so how had Jesus found out?

'His poor sisters must be dreadfully upset,' said James. 'But even so, I don't think they'd want you to take such a risk with your life. They know it isn't safe for you to return immediately. They'll understand.'

The others murmured again amongst themselves about how dangerous it would be. Jesus stood up in front of them, and they suddenly fell silent.

'I'm going to Bethany to see Lazarus and I want you to come with me.'

The disciples glanced from one to the other and knew that this was final. Jesus really meant what he said, and in spite of the danger he was determined to go – accompanied or not! The Pharisees would be watching out for them, and if they were arrested they might be killed. What should the disciples do?

Thomas boldly stepped forward and faced Jesus.

'If you're going then we'll all go too,' he said. 'Even if we all die together!'

The others voiced their agreement, and soon the little company set off on the long walk to Bethany, laughing and joking in an attempt to cover up their fear.

It was difficult walking on the stony roads and it was another two days before they reached Bethany. Nearing the town they met a woman and asked her for news of Lazarus.

'Haven't you heard?' she exclaimed. 'He died four days ago! Mary and Martha's house is full of relatives and friends who have come to mourn with them.'

'How are Mary and Martha?' asked Jesus, concerned.

'Oh, they're dreadfully unhappy,' replied the woman.

'They did everything they could for him – but it was no use. I'm going to their house now, so I'll tell them that you are here, if you want me to.'

'Thank you,' said Jesus, 'that would be very kind.'

She hurried on ahead, and Jesus followed slowly with his disciples. They were amazed, wondering how he had known that Lazarus had died.

When the woman arrived at Mary and Martha's, she told the grieving sisters that Jesus had arrived in Bethany. Mary was surrounded by friends and simply nodded when she heard the news, but Martha was able to slip out of the house. She ran to meet Jesus, hoping to talk with him alone.

Even though she was still very sad at her brother's death, Martha was glad to see Jesus. But there was something she needed to ask him.

'Why did it take so long for you to come? Lazarus was your dear friend – and yet you didn't hurry when we sent a message that he was ill! If you'd been here, I'm sure my brother wouldn't have died.'

Jesus didn't speak but simply held her hands in his, so that Martha could feel the strength in them. She gazed up into his face as she spoke.

'It's not too late – not even now! I know that God will answer your prayers. All you have to do is ask . . .'

'Martha,' Jesus smiled, squeezing her fingers in sympathy, 'don't be so distressed! I promise you that Lazarus is going to live.'

Martha thought this over for a minute.

'I understand what you're trying to tell me,' she stammered. 'Lazarus is going to rise on the Last Day when we are all gathered together again. Yes, I know that.'

But to her surprise Jesus shook his head.

'That isn't what I meant.' He gazed at her very seriously. 'Martha, I am the Resurrection and the Life – anyone who believes in me will live forever! Even when they die here on earth they will go to heaven to live with me there. Then they will be with me forever.'

Jesus gave her some time to think about what he'd said and then asked, 'Now do you understand?'

'I think so,' Martha frowned thoughtfully. 'I know you are the Messiah, the one whom our people have been waiting for so long. And I believe you are the Son of God and you have power over everything.'

Jesus smiled down at her.

'Today you will see God's glory,' he promised, knowing that she really meant what she told him. Then he suddenly changed his tone. 'Where's Mary?'

'She's still in the house,' Martha answered, peering back down the narrow, sunlit street to the white-washed house where Mary was waiting. 'I was able to slip out without anyone seeing me, but Mary had friends all around her. I'll go and tell her you're here and asking for her. She may be able to get here unnoticed.'

Martha turned and hurried homewards. Mary was still in the same room, surrounded by women who were weeping and wailing.

'Jesus is just down the road,' Martha whispered, so that only her sister could hear her. 'He's asking for you.'

Mary stood up, glancing at the other women. At that moment they had their backs to her so she slipped quietly out of the room. If no one had seen her, she could be alone with Jesus for a while, she thought.

However, she hadn't been fast enough! One of the women turned around and saw her, just as she was disappearing through the doorway.

'Mary's just left the house,' she said, nudging her friend. 'She must be going to Lazarus's tomb to weep again.'

Immediately they called to the other women.

'Come quickly! Mary has gone to weep at the tomb again! We mustn't let her go off on her own – come on, let's follow her!'

Martha tried to stop them, but they were making so much noise they didn't hear her! So shrugging her shoulders she followed the noisy group of people to the place where Mary and Jesus were talking.

Meanwhile, Mary had reached the spot where Jesus was waiting. She knelt down in front of him, tears streaming down her cheeks.

'It's good to see you, Lord – but if you'd have come sooner my brother would still be alive!'

Jesus could see how sad and upset she was. Remembering the many happy times he had stayed with his friends at Bethany, how they had laughed and joked or just sat and talked together, he could well understand how miserable Mary felt. Now that Lazarus was dead, things would never be the same again. Tears came to Jesus' eyes and he wept.

'Where have you buried him?' Jesus asked her gently, and Mary led him to where Lazarus lay.

Lazarus's tomb was a cave in the hillside with a large stone rolled across the entrance to seal it. The disciples, the weeping relatives, and Martha – who had by now caught up – all followed.

'Why does he want to look at the tomb?' someone asked, puzzled.

'Surely he doesn't want to go in to see Lazarus' body – not after four days!'

Others spoke bitterly behind his back.

'What sort of a friend was he?' they muttered. 'He has made blind people see, but he couldn't even heal his own friend! And he is supposed to have such powers! I heard he didn't even bother to come when he knew Lazarus was sick.'

Jesus heard, but took no notice of what people were saying. He stood in front of the cave and spoke to some men standing in the crowd.

'Take the stone away,' he ordered.

When she heard this, Martha rushed up to him and clutched hold of his arm.

'Jesus, why do you want the stone rolled away?' she gasped. 'He has been dead for four days so there'll be a nasty smell! It won't be very nice for any of us.'

Looking down at her worried face, Jesus smiled and shook his head.

'Martha, I know what I'm doing. Didn't I tell you earlier that if you believed in me you'd see God's glory?'

'Yes, Lord,' she whispered, her eyes open wide.

'Then trust me and do as I ask,' he responded. 'Take away the stone.'

The four men glanced at Martha, undecided as to what they should do. She nodded to them.

'Do as he says,' was all she said.

The crowd was silent as they edged forward, craning their necks to catch a glimpse of the men struggling with the heavy stone at the entrance to the cave. All the time this was happening, Jesus prayed to God.

At last, the entrance to the cave was open! Some of the people surged forwards, eager to see what would happen next. Others hung back nervously – and one or two actually ran away and hid themselves behind a clump of trees! They certainly didn't want to look inside Lazarus's tomb!

Suddenly, Jesus' voice rang out.

'Lazarus!' he commanded, 'Come out!'

The people in the crowd gasped. What was this man saying? They all knew Lazarus was dead – they'd attended his funeral four days earlier. He couldn't possibly still be alive – and anyway, that heavy stone would have stopped any air entering the tomb, so no one could breathe in there. No, it was impossible. Jesus may have been able to help blind and lame people, but no one could bring the dead back to life!

Even as these thoughts flashed through the minds of those watching, something moved inside the cave. Startled cries escaped from everyone's lips. The people who had craned forward backed away hurriedly, treading on the more nervous people in their fright and haste!

A low gasp went up from the crowd. A figure shuffled out of the tomb and stood before them!

It was wrapped in white grave clothes, with bandages on its hands and feet and a white cloth covering its head. Was it a ghost – or could it be Lazarus brought back from the dead?

Then came a sudden silence as Jesus signalled to the four men who had earlier moved the stone.

'Untie him and let him go.'

The men glanced at one another but not one of them moved. They were too frightened to go near the ghostly figure!

But Mary and Martha didn't hesitate. They rushed forward and began to untie the bandages.

Soon Lazarus stood in front of them for all to see. He was alive and well, walking and talking and laughing! Some of the people reached out to touch him – timidly at first, and then more boldly as they determined he wasn't a ghost but was truly alive!

Then everyone began to talk at once. They ran off excitedly in different directions to tell anyone they met about the miracle they had seen with their own eyes. Lazarus had been raised from the dead!

It was a long time before Mary, Martha and Lazarus were alone with Jesus and his disciples. As they walked back to Bethany, they thanked God for the wonderful miracle that had brought their brother and friend back to them from the dead.

An expensive waste

It had been a long day for everybody. Jesus had been walking with his friends and talking to the crowds of people they had met around Bethany. Meanwhile, Mary and Martha had spent the day preparing a special meal for the men, who had now returned and were relaxing, lying on low couches and sipping cool drinks. They were reflecting on the events of the day and asking Jesus about some of his stories as they looked forward to the food the two women were preparing.

In the kitchen, Martha was almost ready, putting the final touches to the dishes she so enjoyed preparing. She was an excellent cook who enjoyed making delicious meals, especially for Jesus, and, as she couldn't be with him as much as she would have liked, she had decided a long time ago that this was where she could play her special part in Jesus' work. To carry on with his teaching and travelling, Jesus had to eat properly, so whenever Jesus was in Bethany Martha made sure that he was welcomed to her house where she would do her best to cook him something special. This was Matha's way of showing her deep love for Jesus.

Mary, however, didn't share Martha's love of cooking and usually left her to prepare the meals. But today was different! Catering for ten people was a big job, and she had willingly given Martha her help. But as soon as the men had returned, Mary disappeared from the kitchen. Martha glanced up from her work to find herself alone and sighed as she continued. She thought Mary had gone into the room, where the men were waiting, to tell them that the meal was almost ready. When she returned, they'd carry the food in together.

However, Mary wasn't in the room with the men. On leaving the kitchen she'd hurried to her room. All day an idea had been forming in her head and now the time had come for her to carry out her plan. She also loved Jesus and had often wondered how to show him that love in her own special way. It was easy for Martha, with her cooking. She was such a good cook and Jesus often said how tasty her meals were. But Mary was different. She was quiet, preferring to sit at Jesus' feet and listen to him talk than do anything else. That was often difficult though, when the disciples were around. They felt she should stay in the background and not be so close to him. But Jesus had so much to say and always had time to answer her many questions. Besides, he treated her differently from the way other men treated her. He made her feel she was important and that he cared for her.

How though could she show her love for Jesus? That was the question she had often asked herself, and today she had thought of an answer. All day the idea had grown and now she was going to act.

Lying on a table near her bed was a white bottle of perfume with a blue ribbon. Gently she picked up the bottle and carefully placed the ribbon over her head. Tidying her hair she left the room and headed, not for the kitchen, but for the room where Jesus and his disciples sat.

A few noticed her come in but returned to their conversation when they saw she wasn't carrying any food. They paid no more attention to her, except to wonder why she'd come into the room empty-handed. Why didn't she return to the kitchen and hurry up with their meal – they were hungry!

If Mary guessed what they were thinking, she didn't show it. Without looking to either right or left she walked straight up to the couch where Jesus was lying and knelt at his feet.

Mary was now the centre of attention and the disciples were puzzled. Mary had never behaved this way before; perhaps she was ill. The buzz of conversation dropped to a whisper as they watched.

'What's she doing?' Peter asked someone near him.

No one answered immediately as Mary lifted the ribbon from around her neck and carefully opened the bottle of perfume.

'She's just going to pour a little perfume on Jesus' feet,' John whispered. 'I don't see why she's making such a scene, though.'

'Wait a minute,' said Judas sharply a second or two later. 'It's not just a few drops, she's poured the whole bottle over his feet!'

Some of the disciples gasped while others were speechless. They'd never seen anything like it before. Mary had used a whole bottle of perfume! As it trickled over his hot dusty feet, the sweet smelling scent floated into the air and filled the room. Jesus sighed contentedly, cooled and refreshed, but his friends could only stare, stunned. This was too much!

But there was more to come, Mary hadn't finished! As they stared, she slowly began to release her long, dark hair.

This was unheard of! Women weren't allowed to wear their hair loose in public or when men were present. Had Mary gone mad? What was she thinking of? She knew the rules and yet here she was in a room full of men and it didn't matter to her one little bit.

Mary knew exactly what she was doing. Her hair was now undone and fell freely down her back, shining in the glow of the lamps. Kneeling low at Jesus' feet, she wiped the perfume from them with her hair, using soft, loving strokes. Away came the dust and dirt which had clung to Jesus' feet as he had walked that day. Happy and content, Mary knew that at last she had found a way of showing Jesus how much she cared.

But the disciples weren't happy and whispered angrily amongst themselves.

'Did you see that?' whispered John. 'A whole bottle of perfume wasted.'

'Why use it all?' questioned another. 'What is the usual amount to use? A few drops, that's all, to cool a person's feet. And what does Mary use? A whole bottle!'

'She should have used a cheaper perfume if she had decided she was going to use so much,' added Judas. 'You can tell by its scent that it is very expensive. Someone should tell her how wicked she's been in wasting it all.'

The others agreed as they sniffed the air. The scent of the perfume still lingered in the room.

'She must have paid a great deal of money for it,' said James. 'Mary hasn't got money to throw away like that. I'm sure she could have spent it more wisely on something else.'

'It would have done more good if she had sold it and given the money to us,' agreed Judas. 'If she'd asked my advice, that's what I would have told her. I'd have made sure that the poor were helped with the money . . .'

'What more could you expect from a woman?'

The mutterings of the disciples grew louder and louder as they became angrier and angrier with Mary. Not one of them could understand why she had done such a silly thing. As they muttered, Mary sat silently at Jesus' feet. Her hair, still loose and smelling of perfume, fell in thick strands over her shoulders. She was puzzled by the disciples' talk and her peaceful, happy expression was now confused. Why were they looking at her in such an angry way? She hadn't done or said anything to them.

At that moment, Jesus, who hadn't spoken at all, held up his hand for silence.

'What's the matter?' he asked, looking around at his disciples. 'A moment ago everyone was chatting quite happily together and now suddenly you're all grumbling. What's wrong?'

The disciples glanced from one to the other, shuffling their feet as they wondered who would speak first. Then Judas stepped forward.

'It's Mary,' he blurted out. 'And what she's just done.'

'Mary?' asked Jesus surprised. 'What about her? Is something wrong?'

The disciples gazed at one another in amazement. What did Jesus mean? Didn't he know?

'Wrong!' exclaimed James. 'She's just wasted a whole bottle of perfume.'

'And expensive perfume too,' added Peter. 'It would have cost a whole year's wages to pay for that bottle and now it's all gone – just like that.' He clicked his fingers together sharply.

'We could have done so much with that money,' added Judas. 'We would have bought food and clothing for the poor and helped many, many people.'

'But now we can't,' James grumbled. 'Both money and perfume are gone – because she wasted it.'

He pointed angrily at Mary and the other men glared at her. She remained at Jesus' feet, but her head drooped slightly so she couldn't see their faces. Her fine idea had ended in disaster. All she had wanted to do was show Jesus how much she loved him and now it had all been turned upside down. Jesus would think her a fool – a wasteful, uncaring fool, as his friends thought. Everything had turned out wrong. He hadn't said anything to her so he must be very angry with her. What could she say? How could she explain? She wished she could just disappear . . .

Her thoughts were interrupted as Jesus rose to his feet. She didn't dare raise her head but continued staring at the floor. Then Jesus spoke in a stern voice.

'Leave her alone. She has done a lovely thing for me.'

Mary looked up with tears of relief and joy in her eyes. He wasn't angry with her at all! He was speaking to the men – he did understand; she should have known all along that he would! Jesus always understood. He put out his hand and helped a smiling Mary to her feet.

'But Jesus,' said Judas, '. . . you don't understand.'

'It's you who doesn't understand, Judas,' Jesus replied. 'Mary spent a great deal of money on that perfume and she used it, not on herself, but on me, to cool my tired feet. Then she wiped it away, not with a rough towel, but with her soft hair. It was simply her way of showing that she loves me – and a very beautiful way too, I think.'

'We know that,' said Peter impatiently, 'but she could have sold the perfume – or given us the money before she'd bought it. You're always telling us to help the poor, and we could have helped so many people with that money. That's how Mary could have shown how much she loves you!'

'There will always be poor people,' said Jesus. 'It is important for you to help them and you can do that any time you like, but you won't always have me.'

The disciples realised that Jesus was trying to tell them something important and so they listened hard, trying to understand what he was saying.

'People have different ways of showing that they care for others,' Jesus continued. 'This is the way Mary has chosen to show she cares for me and it's not your place to say she's wrong.'

Mary decided it was time to go. She left the room and hurried to her bedroom to re-arrange her hair. Except for the faint smell of perfume that lingered, things seemed no different. But Mary felt different inside.

She returned to the kitchen to help her sister with the meal which was now ready to be carried in.

'Oh, there you are,' said Martha. 'I was just going to call you. Everything's ready.' Suddenly she sniffed the air, puzzled. 'What's that smell? It's lovely.'

Mary smiled mysteriously. 'I'll tell you later,' she whispered and gathered up some plates.

Meanwhile Jesus had sat down again on the couch. He stared at his feet for a few moments in silence and then glanced at his disciples.

'There is a deeper meaning to what Mary has done today,' he said. 'I'm not going to tell you now, but perhaps one day you'll understand.'

The disciples were more confused than ever. There were so many things Jesus said that they didn't understand, and here was yet another mystery. What deeper meaning could there be in Mary pouring a whole bottle of perfume over Jesus' feet?

'Let me just say this,' said Jesus, seeing their puzzled faces. 'What Mary has done today will be retold by many people in the future and she will be remembered for years to come for her kindness to me.'

At that moment, Martha and Mary entered the room with the food. The disciples watched Mary closely and wondered about her.

The Lord is risen!

It was all over – it was finished! All their hopes and dreams were dashed – their expectations over. The small group of women stood heartbroken beside the cross on which Jesus had been crucified.

The events of the last few days had happened so fast. Was it only a week ago that Jesus had ridden into Jerusalem on a donkey with the whole city cheering and waving palm branches, hailing him as a king?

What a difference a week had made! For yesterday those same crowds hadn't cheered Jesus but had shouted for Pilate to have him killed! Why had they changed their minds so quickly?

Salome and the two Marys didn't know – they didn't understand anything any more! In their eyes nothing had altered – Jesus was still the same person who had healed the lame, made the blind see and told the wonderful stories that so many people were keen to hear. But everything had suddenly turned upside down – Jesus' enemies had won and he had been killed. But what had he done to hurt any of them, the three friends wondered? Why did they hate him so much that they wanted him dead?

The women stood silently, gazing up at the limp body on the cross. How empty they felt! While he had been alive, Jesus had treated them so differently from the way men usually did – he had behaved as if they were loved and wanted, as if their feelings mattered to him in the same way as those of his male disciples did. No wonder the women loved him so much! They couldn't face the thought of life going on in the same way as it had before they met him!

The two Marys and Salome hadn't spoken much during the long hours that Jesus had hung dying on the cross. It had been terrible watching the crowds laughing and jeering at him.

'You performed great miracles for others!' one man had

shouted. 'Why can't you save yourself?'

His friends laughed as they sauntered over to jeer at the other two men who were crucified on either side of Jesus.

All day, Mary had searched the crowds, looking for Peter and the other disciples, but she could only find John.

'Perhaps the others are afraid that they'll be arrested too,' suggested Salome when Mary asked if she had seen them.

'Perhaps,' Mary murmured, 'but it doesn't seem right to leave him alone now, no matter what the danger! I couldn't stay away from him – not at this moment – not ever!'

The others agreed, their eyes red from crying, their hearts aching with sorrow.

At that moment a soldier marched up to Jesus and pushed a spear into his side, checking to see if he were dead. The women turned away quickly, closing their eyes and shuddering as if it had entered their own bodies. When at last they opened their eyes and peered back at the cross, they realised that Jesus' suffering was over. He was dead, and the soldiers were busy taking the cross down and laying it on the ground.

One of the soldiers noticed the women there and marched over to them, frowning and waving his arms. 'You women go home!' he shouted. 'There's nothing more for you to see. Off you go!'

Slowly the women backed away, but when the soldier returned to his work, they stopped in a little huddle and watched. Although the soldier glanced back at them from time to time, he didn't shoo them away again. He didn't care if a few women wanted to watch what they were doing. He didn't care at all. The sooner this job was finished, the sooner he could go home!

A few minutes later the women noticed a man coming up the hill, striding beside a soldier dressed in an officer's uniform. The soldiers also saw them approaching and jumped to attention when the officer drew near. As the officer began to speak, the women crept nearer so they could hear the conversation.

'This man is Joseph of Arimathea,' the officer barked. 'He has asked Pilate for the body of Jesus of Nazareth.' He glanced around. 'Is this him?'

'Yes, sir,' replied one of the soldiers, standing smartly to attention.

'What do you want to do with the body?' asked the officer, turning to Joseph.

'There's a tomb down there in the garden which is ready to be used,' said Joseph, pointing down the hill. 'I'd like the soldiers to help me carry the body down to it.'

The officer turned back to his men and gave instructions to two of the soldiers.

'Carry the body to this tomb,' he ordered 'and be quick about it.'

Joseph nodded. 'Yes – the Sabbath Day will be starting soon and the body must be in the tomb before it begins.'

The soldiers mumbled and grumbled amongst themselves about Jews and the Sabbath Day as they picked up the body of Jesus. They wrapped it in the white linen sheet that Joseph had brought with him and then followed Joseph down the hill, carrying the body. The other soldiers and the officer marched back to the city, leaving the women on their own.

'Come on, hurry!' whispered Salome. 'We must follow Joseph and find out where this tomb is . . .'

They followed the men at a safe distance, taking great care that no-one saw them. 'We won't have time to anoint his body today,' whispered Mary. 'It's nearly the Sabbath Day already. We'll come back on Sunday, once we know where the body is.'

They followed Joseph and the soldiers to the garden and hid behind some trees, while the men carried the body into a cave. Almost immediately, the soldiers reappeared empty handed.

'Help me pull this stone across the entrance!' Joseph called to them. 'I want to make sure this tomb is sealed properly.'

The three men heaved and pushed an enormous stone until it covered the opening of the cave. Then, still breathing hard and rubbing their scratched hands, the soldiers ambled off. Joseph glanced about him, checked again that the stone was secure, and then he too hurried away.

'We'd better hurry home too,' said Salome as they crept out of their hiding place. 'It's getting very late.'

As they hurried away, Mary glanced back over her shoulder.

'His body will be safe in there,' she murmured. 'No one could move that heavy stone by themselves.'

The Sabbath was at last over. Jews weren't allowed to do any work at all on that day, and oh! how the hours had dragged for the women as they sat silently, wrapped up in their own sadness. Over and over again, they thought about the events of the last three years – the stories Jesus had told, his loving smile and voice – all the things they would never see or hear any more! Why, oh why had such a dreadful thing happened?

That night Mary found it impossible to sleep. She tossed and turned for hours until at last she gave up. It was no use, she decided. She might as well get out of bed and do something.

Lighting the lamp on the table so she could see in the dark, she began to collect everything she would need later. Just as she finished, she heard a gentle knock at her front door. Mary quickly opened it, wondering who could be calling at her home in the middle of the night.

Joanna stood there, her finger to her lips. There were dark shadows under her eyes and Mary could tell that she hadn't had much sleep either.

'Can we come in?' she whispered, and as Mary stepped back Joanna crept in, followed by several other women. In their hands were jars of ointments like the one Mary had filled.

'None of us could sleep,' explained Joanna. 'As we were

passing we noticed your light burning, so we knew you were awake too.'

'We're going to the tomb now,' confided her friend. 'There's no reason why we should wait any longer.'

Mary agreed, and wrapping a shawl around her shoulders, followed the other women into the dark street that led to the garden.

Once they were away from the houses, Mary suddenly broke the silence.

'I've just been thinking,' she said. 'How are we going to move that heavy stone? We saw how much trouble those soldiers had in pushing it into place.'

'Oh, I never thought of that!' one of the women groaned.

'We'll just have to try,' Joanna told them firmly. 'There are more of us, so we may be able to move it if we all push together.'

As they reached the garden, Mary who was leading, stopped suddenly.

'What's the matter?' asked the other Mary, who had bumped into her.

'Look!' she replied, pointing. 'Someone's been here already. The stone's been rolled away!'

'It can't be . . .' gasped Joanna. They all rushed forward to get a closer look. But it was true! In the silvery moonlight which streamed across the shadowed garden, they could all see the clear dark outline of the tomb, its open entrance yawning darkly! The large stone that the soldiers had struggled with was lying on its side by the edge of the cave!

Without thinking, the women rushed into the tomb . . . but it was empty! The body of Jesus, which had been wrapped in the white sheet, was gone!

'Who could have done this?' cried Mary, uncertain whether to be angry or to cry. This was too much! For Jesus to have been killed was bad enough – but for his body to have been stolen – why, that was unbearable! Why would anyone want to do such a thing? It all seemed like some sort of horrible nightmare!

As the little group stood huddled miserably together in the tomb, an extraordinary thing happened. Suddenly, two bright shining figures appeared as if from nowhere! As the terrified women backed towards the door of the tomb, one of the mysterious figures held up a hand and spoke:

'Don't be afraid,' he smiled. 'We're not going to hurt you. What are you doing here?'

Mary at last found her voice and stammered nervously.

'We . . . we've come to an . . . anoint Jesus' body. But . . . but he isn't here.'

'Of course he isn't here,' the figure laughed. 'This place is for the dead. Jesus isn't dead – he's alive!'

'Alive?' chorused the women, coming closer. This news was so unexpected that they quite forgot how frightened they had been! They stared at the two strangers in complete astonishment.

'Yes,' said the other figure. 'Don't you remember? He told you that he must die, but that three days later he would rise again. Well, today is the third day.'

The women looked at one another, trying to remember Jesus saying those words. When they turned back, the shining figures had gone – disappearing as silently as they had come!

Joanna was the first to recover sufficiently to speak.

'I remember Jesus saying that . . .' she said slowly '. . . but I didn't understand what he meant at the time and I didn't like to ask.'

'Is it possible that he could be alive?' Mary whispered tentatively. She sighed, her tear-stained eyes filling again. 'Oh . . . oh, if only it could be true!'

'He raised Lazarus from the dead,' the other Mary stated. 'So why couldn't he do the same for himself?'

The women nodded in agreement, becoming more and more excited as the incredible news slowly sank in. Their beloved Jesus wasn't dead after all. He was alive!

'We can't just stand here doing nothing,' said Mary suddenly. 'We must go and tell someone – anyone!'

'Let's go and find the disciples!' cried Joanna, making for the doorway. 'They'll be as excited with the news as we are.'

Mary followed her. 'Yes,' she agreed, rushing excitedly ahead. 'Come on everyone – I know where they are! Hurry up – let's not waste any more time!'

Joyfully they ran to a house in the town and hammered on the door. Thomas opened it a tiny way and peeped out. He sighed with relief when he realised who it was.

'Oh, it's only you,' he breathed. 'Come in quickly and close the door. I thought you were Roman soldiers coming to arrest us.'

Seated in the room were some more of the disciples. They looked tired and nervous, jumping at the slightest sound.

'What are you doing here?' snapped Andrew. 'The soldiers could have followed you and found out where we are . . .'

'Well, they haven't,' Mary panted impatiently. 'Everyone is still asleep. But listen . . .'

'Well, what are you doing here?' Thomas interrupted. He was pale and strained looking – and obviously still very frightened. Mary caught hold of his arm.

'Give me a chance to speak, will you, Thomas! We've got the most wonderful news to tell you – Jesus is alive!'

The disciples simply stared open-mouthed at the women.

'Don't tell lies like that,' one snorted when he'd finally found his voice. 'Jesus is dead. I wasn't there, but I know he died on Friday on a cross. He's dead and that's all there is to it!'

'He died on a cross, yes – but he has risen!' cried Joanna.

'We went to the tomb a little while ago,' Mary broke in nervously. 'But when we arrived, the tomb was empty! Then we saw two . . . two angels and they told us that he had risen from the dead!'

'Angels!' cried James in disgust. 'You expect us to believe that ordinary people – ordinary women – like you, saw angels?'

'Yes,' said Joanna defiantly, her eyes shining. 'It's true.'

'You've been dreaming,' scoffed John. 'Jesus is dead and that's that. There's nothing we can do about it, and no amount of wishful thinking will bring him back. Now go away before someone hears you and finds us. We're not interested in your silly stories.'

'But the body isn't there,' cried Mary anxiously. 'Go and look for yourself. It's gone!'

'Gone?' exclaimed Peter, standing up so quickly that he knocked over his chair. 'Someone must have stolen it!'

'But the angels told us . . .'

'Forget about the angels,' cried James. 'What we need to know is – what have they done with the body?'

'But . . .'

'You'd better go,' snapped John, opening the door. 'The whole town will be awake soon, and the soldiers will find us.'

'Don't you believe anything we've said?' Mary demanded, as the other women filed out of the house.

'No we don't,' growled Thomas, speaking for them all. 'I can't imagine why you made up such a story. Angels indeed!'

With that John closed the door in their faces.

Joanna turned to the other women. 'I'm going home,' she told them. 'I feel so tired and confused . . . I was so sure – but now . . .' her voice trailed off into silence.

The others nodded dumbly. They knew exactly what Joanna meant; they all felt the same. One by one they separated, heading off to their homes to try and get some sleep – all, that is, except for Mary Magdalene. 'I can't have dreamt it all!' she muttered to herself, turning to look back at the silent garden. 'It all seemed so real!'

She frowned, thinking deeply, and then exclaimed: 'It's no good – I'm going back! I have to be sure that Jesus' body isn't there!'

And all alone, she made her way towards the tomb . . .

After the women had gone, the disciples had begun to argue excitedly.

'Whatever were those women trying to do?' asked Thomas. 'Making up such an incredible story? Who did they think they were trying to impress?'

'I've never heard of anything like it,' agreed Bartholomew. 'What do you think, Peter?'

Peter scratched his head, his brow furrowed with concentration. After a few minutes, he rose slowly to his feet.

'I'm going to the tomb,' he announced, glancing at his companions, who stared back at him in amazement.

'What?' cried James. 'You don't believe them, do you?'

'I don't know . . .' said Peter thoughtfully. 'They seemed so excited when they came in – they'd certainly seen something strange. Anyway, that's not all that's bothering me.'

The others waited as Peter struggled with his thoughts.

'They said the body was gone. If that's true, then I want to know what's happened to it.'

As Peter headed for the door, Philip grabbed hold of his arm.

'What about the soldiers?' he demanded. 'You might be seen!'

'I'll be careful,' Peter replied.

'Then I'm coming too,' John decided, and the two men disappeared into the night.

They ran along the streets, guided by the moonlight, their minds in a whirl as they tried to make sense of what had happened.

John ran faster than Peter and arrived at the garden first. He stopped sharply when the tomb came into sight – he could see at once that the stone had been rolled aside! The light of the moon cast weird shadows around him, and John halted nervously, afraid to go any further . . .

At that moment Peter arrived, puffing and panting. Without a moment's hesitation he pushed past his companion and stumbled through the opening, his breathing the only sound within the silent tomb. In the cold moonlight which streamed over his shoulder, he could just make out the shape of the winding-sheet lying on the rocky shelf; the cloth which had been wrapped round Jesus' head lay some distance away, tossed carelessly onto the floor.

'So the women were right . . .' Peter murmured under his breath. 'The body isn't here . . .'

John's voice sounded anxiously from the entrance to the cave.

'Can you see anything?' He craned his head around the edge of the opening to get a better look. 'I saw the sheet lying there . . . is there any sign of the body?'

'It's not here,' Peter replied flatly. 'The women were telling the truth. You had better come inside.'

Silently, John stepped into the cave. He stared around him at the emptiness, wondering what could have happened. Had somebody stolen Jesus' body, or – he hardly dared even think it – could Jesus really have risen from the dead? The empty tomb stared back at him.

Peter turned to John, his face pale and bewildered.

'What has happened here?' he whispered, half to his companion and half to himself. 'Can he really be alive?'

John gazed once more at the discarded grave-clothes and

then back at Peter. 'Yes,' he told him, and then again more firmly. 'Yes – I really believe he is!'

And filled with a sudden overwhelming happiness, the two friends rushed back to tell the others the wonderful news.

But in the meantime, what had happened to Mary Magdalene? She had set off to the garden in a great hurry, but the events of the night had tired her so much that she had had to slow down, giving herself a chance to sort out her jumbled thoughts. She had been so sure that Jesus was alive – the angels had said so and the body had gone – but then the disciples had accused her of making it all up! Perhaps she had been so tired that she had fallen asleep – then she might have dreamt it all. Mary sighed – it was all too much to take in. She wasn't the only one to have seen the angels, she told herself crossly – the other women had seen them as well! Surely half a dozen people don't have the same dream! Oh, if only she knew what to think!

By the time she reached the empty tomb, Mary had begun to cry again. She didn't think she had any tears left after the last two days, but now she felt so helpless and confused that they came coursing down her cheeks again. As she stood there, wiping her swollen eyes on the corner of her shawl, she heard a sudden rustling sound and quickly looked around. Her eyes were so full of tears that she couldn't see properly, but in the dim light she could just make out the blurry figure of a man. Hastily she bent her head, trying to dry her eyes.

'Why are you crying?' the man asked, quietly. When Mary didn't answer, he spoke again. 'Who is it that you're looking for?'

Mary sniffed, blew her nose and finally felt able to speak. He must be the gardener, she thought, so perhaps he might know what had happened to the body of her beloved Jesus. She stood up straight, clearing her throat.

'If you've taken him away sir,' she asked timidly, pointing to the empty tomb. 'Please tell me where you've put him. Then I can go and get him and bring him back.'

The stranger was silent for a moment, and when he spoke it was just one word: 'Mary . . .!'

Mary's head flew up instantly! It was not the fact that this man knew her name – it was the way he had said it! Only one man had ever spoken her name in that caring tone of voice –

Jesus! – and at that moment she knew it was him speaking to her! The angels had told the truth – he had risen and she was seeing and talking with him!

A lump came into her throat as she tried to speak.

'Teacher,' she whispered, and stepped forward to touch him. But Jesus held up his hand.

'I don't want you to hold me yet,' he told her. 'You can see me and you know that I'm alive. That must be sufficient for the moment.'

Mary didn't dare take her eyes from his face. She didn't need to touch him to believe that he was alive. She could see and hear him and that was enough!

'I want you to go and tell my disciples that I have risen,' he continued, '. . . and that they'll see me soon.'

Mary nodded, and waited until he had left the garden, watching him all the time. Then she ran to the house where the disciples were hiding – only this time she was laughing and skipping as she ran, her tiredness completely forgotten!

Those men would have to believe her this time! It wasn't a dream – she knew that every word of it was true! And even if they were still just as obstinate – well, she didn't care! Mary knew – what a glorious thing she knew! – and what wonderful news she had to tell everybody!

Part of a team

It was now several years since Mary Magdalene had met with the risen Jesus, and his followers and disciples had started their great mission. They were busy spreading the Good News – that Jesus is always with us. He died so that we too can rise from death to life in heaven with him!

People were still talking about Jesus, and as more and more of them came to believe, they too began to share his teachings with others – the message was far too exciting to keep to themselves!

Paul was one such person. He travelled through many countries telling everyone he met about the love of Jesus. Sometimes he travelled by boat, and other times he walked, and he had many adventures – spreading the Good News wasn't easy work! Often, Paul found that people didn't want to hear what he was teaching – they were happy living their lives as they had always done and didn't want to change. Others didn't agree with Jesus' words and became so angry with Paul that they threw him into prison.

One of Paul's many journeys took him to Greece. He had just arrived in the town of Corinth when he realised he didn't have very much money left. Now Paul travelled a great deal teaching about Jesus, and he had to pay for his transport as well as his food, shelter and clothing. It all cost a lot of money, and to pay for it Paul had to work! He was a tent-maker, and he was very clever and skilled at his trade, making all sorts of leather-goods as well as just tents. If he was going to stay in Corinth, Paul thought, he would have to find a job and earn some money – otherwise he would go hungry and cold!

Walking along a street Paul suddenly stopped and sniffed the air. He grinned as he recognized the familiar smell of leather coming from a nearby doorway, and he knew he had found some fellow tent-makers.

Peering through the doorway, he called out.

'Hello! Is anyone there?'

A few seconds later a man appeared from behind a curtain, which hung at the rear of the dimly lit room.

'Can I help you?' he asked. 'Did you want to buy something?'

'Well, er . . . no,' said Paul. 'I don't want to buy anything. I was passing in the street and smelt the leather – you see, I'm a tent-maker and I'm looking for a job.'

'I see . . .' said the man, stroking his chin as he watched Paul closely. 'You're looking for work here in Corinth?'

Paul nodded. 'I'm Paul, and I've come here to tell people about Jesus Christ. Have you ever heard of him?

As Paul spoke, the man's face broke into a wide grin.

'You're Paul?' he cried excitedly. 'I've heard so much about you! This is wonderful! My wife and I are followers of Jesus too – wait here a minute while I call her!'

He shook the startled Paul by the hand and then rushed out of sight, calling loudly 'Priscilla – Priscilla! You'll never guess who's here!'

'We've heard so much about you,' Priscilla beamed. 'Come

on, Aquila, Paul must be exhausted! Come inside, both of you, and we'll all have something to eat.'

'I must admit this is a surprise,' laughed Paul as they made their way through the shop, where piles of material and tools lay scattered across the work benches. 'I certainly didn't expect a welcome like this!'

'How long have you been in Corinth?' Priscilla asked as they entered the living room.

Paul took a date from the plate she offered before replying.

'I've only just arrived. I knew that the first thing I had to do was earn some money before I began teaching here, and I just chanced to meet Aquila.'

'You were led here by the Lord!' Priscilla told him warmly. 'And of course you can work with us, for as long as you want! But why have you chosen to come to Corinth?'

'I've heard that there are many people here who don't know about Jesus,' Paul replied. 'So I thought I would come and see for myself what is happening.'

Priscilla nodded, a sad expression on her face.

'What you say is true,' she agreed. 'There are so many people here who have never heard of him! Aquila and I do our best but it's such a big city. We need as much help as we can get.'

They sat quietly for a while, thinking of the huge job facing them.

'Have you always lived here in Corinth?' Paul asked after a few moments silence.

'No,' replied Aquila. 'We were living in Italy but the Emperor Claudius ordered all the Jews to leave Rome. As I'm a Jew we had to pack all our belongings and move.'

'We decided to come to Greece,' Priscilla continued, 'and we set up our tent-making business here in Corinth. There's a good trade here because the town is so busy.'

Paul nodded. He had noticed the bustling shops and market-stalls on his walk through the city.

'How long do you think you'll be in Corinth for?' asked Aquila.

'I don't know, but I think it will be a few months at least. I have to find somewhere to live first, though.'

Priscilla and her husband looked at one another. They knew many of the teachings of Jesus, but they could learn so much more from Paul! If he stayed at their house they would be able to talk and share ideas and experiences.

'You must stay with us,' Aquila said firmly. 'You can live here and work with us in our business.'

Paul stared from one to the other.

'Well, that's very kind of you . . .' he faltered. 'I don't want to be a burden . . .'

'You won't be a burden,' Priscilla interrupted. 'We want to hear more about Jesus – so really we'll be helping each other!'

Paul grinned. 'I can see we're going to get on well as a team,' he said. 'We'll all help one another as we work together.'

Paul remained with Priscilla and Aquila for several months – and they did work well together. They were busy at their trade of tent-making, and they also talked about Jesus to anyone in Corinth who would listen. It was exciting to see so many people changing the way they lived after they heard the Good News.

One day as they were stitching a large tent in the work room, Paul spoke seriously to his friends.

'I think it's time I moved on,' he said thoughtfully. 'There are still so many people in other towns and countries who need to hear about Jesus. I think my work here in Corinth is done for the time being.'

'Where are you planning to go?' asked Priscilla, putting down the piece of leather she was stitching.

'I think I'll go by boat to Syria first and then travel home from there,' Paul told her. 'I haven't made definite plans yet.'

Priscilla thought for a moment. 'We could go with you as far as Syria,' she said, 'and stay there when you go on. That way we can go to different towns and tell even more people about Jesus.'

Aquila nodded his head. 'That sounds like a good idea. What do you think Paul?'

'What about your trade?' Paul inquired. 'You may be away for many months.'

'That won't matter,' replied Aquila. 'The workers here are very capable, as you know! They'll manage perfectly well while we're away.'

'Then I agree,' said Paul. 'It's a marvellous idea! You've done so much here in Corinth and I'm sure you'll be just as successful in Syria. As I've said before – we make a fine team!'

So it was agreed. Soon they were packed and sailing for Ephesus, where Priscilla and Aquila disembarked.

'Make sure you write and tell me how you're getting on!' Paul shouted to them as the mooring lines were cast off and the boat pulled away from the shore.

'We will! Have a good voyage and God be with you!'. They stood by the shore and watched the sail disappear over the distant horizon.

At first Priscilla and Aquila missed their friend. The city was strange to them, they didn't know anybody there. They now knew how Paul had felt when he had first come to Corinth, not knowing anybody else. However they soon settled down and started to preach to the people about Jesus.

They were in the synagogue one day when they heard a young man preaching about Jesus. Stopping to listen they were impressed by the way he spoke.

'He's a good preacher, isn't he?' Priscilla whispered. 'But I don't think he knows the whole story of Jesus.'

Aquila nodded. 'I was just thinking the very same,' he said. 'He hasn't mentioned the power of the Holy Spirit at all. Do you think we should talk with him about it?'

Priscilla agreed, so when the young man had finished speaking, they walked over to him.

'My name is Apollos,' he said after they had introduced themselves.

'We were interested in your teaching,' Aquila began, 'We're followers of Jesus as well . . .'

'I'm pleased to meet you,' beamed Apollos. 'I have heard so much about Jesus and his life.'

'We realise that,' said Priscilla. 'It shows in what you have to say. However, we feel that you only think of Jesus as a great teacher who once lived – as a man from history. We'd like to talk with you and share how we feel about Jesus – that he's a real person who is alive and as important today as when he was on this earth.'

Apollos glanced from one to the other curiously.

'I'd like to hear what you have to say,' he said. 'Yes – I'd be interested in what you can tell me about Jesus.'

He returned with them to their home and they talked together for hours about Jesus, his life and his teachings. Apollos, who thought he knew everything about Jesus, was amazed! He listened carefully and asked many questions. Priscilla and Aquila also told him about the Holy Spirit who had been sent as a helper by God. This was all completely new to Apollos.

After three hours he leaned back in his chair, sighing deeply.

'Everything you've told me is so new and exciting!' he said. 'I've learnt so much from you. It's wonderful!'

'You can go and preach anywhere now,' said Aquila. 'You speak boldly and now that you know the whole story you will be able to spread the Good News far and wide.'

'Oh, I do hope so!' said Apollos eagerly. 'In fact, I had dreams of going to Achaia, but . . .' He stopped.

'But what?' asked Priscilla.

'I don't know anyone there,' Apollos blushed.

'That's not a problem,' laughed Priscilla. 'We have friends there. We'll write and let them know that you're coming – they'll be interested in what you have to say. I'm sure they'll make you really welcome!'

Apollos grinned, relaxed and happy. Now he was even more eager to begin his travels.

Several days later he left Ephesus for Achaia, knowing that a letter was already on its way ahead of him, introducing him to more people who would soon be his friends.

Priscilla and Aquila left Ephesus too, and travelled huge distances as they taught about Jesus. Together they had some exciting adventures and also some nasty experiences – but nothing stopped them in their work. Often they received letters from Paul, and they also heard good news of Apollos from Achaia. They prayed frequently for their friends – and for those who didn't yet know the Good News of the love of Jesus. And all the time they knew that others were praying for them as well.